SOURCE CRITICISM

CASCADE COMPANIONS

The Christian theological tradition provides an embarrassment of riches: from Scripture to modern scholarship, we are blessed with a vast and complex theological inheritance. And yet this feast of traditional riches is too frequently inaccessible to the general reader.

The Cascade Companions series addresses the challenge by publishing books that combine academic rigor with broad appeal and readability. They aim to introduce nonspecialist readers to that vital storehouse of authors, documents, themes, histories, arguments, and movements that comprise this heritage with brief yet compelling volumes.

A SELECTION OF TITLES IN THIS SERIES:

The Canaanites by Mary Ellen Buck
David: A Man after God's Own Heart by Benjamin J. M. Johnson
Approaching Job by Andrew Zack Lewis
Jeremiah by Jack R. Lundblom
The Book of the Twelve by Beth M. Stovell and David J. Fuller
Amos, Hosea, and Micah by Jack R. Lundbom
Reading Mark by Kelly R. Iverson
Reading Luke by Frank Dicken
Jesus and the Empire of God by Warren Carter
Reading Acts by Joshua W. Jipp
The First Christian Letters by Rafael Rodríguez
Reading Philippians by Nijay K. Gupta
A Companion to Philemon by Lewis Brogdon
The Rule of Faith by Everett Ferguson
Origen by Ronald E. Heine
Practicing Lament by Rebekah Eklund
Mimetic Theory and Biblical Interpretation by Michael Hardin
Theological Interpretation of Scripture by Stephen E. Fowl
Handel's Messiah by Gregory S. Athnos
Understanding the Freewill Controversy by Thomas Talbott

SOURCE CRITICISM

JOEL S. BADEN

 CASCADE *Books* • Eugene, Oregon

SOURCE CRITICISM

Cascade Companions

Cascade Books
An Imprint of Wipf and Stock Publishers
199 W. 8th Ave., Suite 3
Eugene, OR 97401

www.wipfandstock.com

PAPERBACK ISBN: 978-1-6667-6409-3
HARDCOVER ISBN: 978-1-6667-6410-9
EBOOK ISBN: 978-1-6667-6411-6

Cataloguing-in-Publication data:

Names: Baden, Joel S., 1977– [author].

Title: Source criticism / by Joel S. Baden.

Description: Eugene, OR: Cascade Books, 2024 | Series: Cascade Companions | Includes bibliographical references.

Identifiers: ISBN 978-1-6667-6409-3 (paperback) | ISBN 978-1-6667-6410-9 (hardcover) | ISBN 978-1-6667-6411-6 (ebook)

Subjects: LCSH: Documentary hypothesis (Pentateuchal criticism) | Bible.—Pentateuch—Criticism, interpretation, etc. | E document (Biblical criticism) | J document (Biblical criticism) | P document (Biblical criticism) | Bible.—O.T.—Pentateuch—Criticism, Redaction | Bible—Hermeneutics

Classification: BS1225.52 NUMBER 2024 (paperback) | BS1225.52 (ebook)

VERSION NUMBER 05/17/24

CONTENTS

Introduction | 1

1. Early Theories: Sources, Fragments, Supplements | 13
2. Defining the Sources | 36
3. The Classical Period of Source Criticism | 58
4. Complications: Addition and Subtraction | 78
5. Reimagining Source Criticism | 98
6. A Return to the Sources | 121

Conclusion | 142

Bibliography | 147

INTRODUCTION

"Source criticism" is a misnomer. Something of a strange way to open a book titled *Source Criticism*, admittedly, but it's worth putting the issue on the table from the beginning. Generally, when we talk about various types of "criticisms," what we are describing is a set of questions. Form criticism looks into the form of a textual unit; tradition criticism asks about the traditions underlying the text; feminist criticism centers the role of women in the text and the history of its interpretation. In each of these, the type of criticism—form, tradition, feminist—determines the course of the critical inquiry. But this is not the case with source criticism. In source criticism, the discovery of sources isn't the aim of the approach; it is, rather, the result.

As we will see, no one ever picked up the biblical text and thought, "I'm going to find myself some sources in here—now how should I do that?" Rather, they picked up the text and thought, "Well, this is odd—why does the text look like this?" And the answer that they came up with, in all sorts of variations, was that the most likely reason that the text reads the way that it does is because it was not originally written by a single author at one time. Rather, it is the product of the combination of disparate literary pieces, from different hands. Sources are the conclusion, not the starting point, of the analysis.

Another way that source criticism differs from other types of criticism is in its scope and applicability. Every text is susceptible to form criticism—every text participates in a literary form. Every text builds on traditions. Every text can be subject to a feminist reading, or a queer or post-colonial critical lens. (I mean *every* text, biblical or not, ancient or modern.) But not every text is open to a source-critical inquiry—especially if what we mean is that the text was created out of multiple distinct original sources. It is only those texts that demonstrate certain literary qualities, certain unexpected oddities—only those texts that make someone ask, "Why does the text look like this?"—that demand this sort of analysis.

It is for this reason that "source criticism" almost always refers to the analysis of the literary history of the Pentateuch in particular. It was this corpus that caught the attention of early biblical scholars, insofar as it was in the Pentateuch that the most prominent literary oddities were most readily identifiable. Why does the Pentateuch look like this? Eventually, the most common answer would be "sources." But the same couldn't be said for just any text. Sources were the explanation for the Pentateuch's unique literary shape. A different corpus, with different literary qualities, wouldn't—indeed, shouldn't—result in the same literary history.

Of course, any text's literary history may be investigated. But to call such investigations "source criticism" is not quite accurate. Better, perhaps, to talk of "literary-historical criticism," where the guiding question is "how did this text come to be?" Sometimes, as with the Pentateuch, the answer might be "sources!" But sometimes it will be "single authorship," or perhaps "single authorship with a few later additions." So here too we must be careful with our terms. As we will discuss in the following chapters, "sources" refers to a very specific type of literary history. Later additions to an extant text are not technically, or necessarily, "sources."

All of this is to say: the term "source criticism" can be misleading. If it is used in its most narrow sense, to refer to the claim that the Pentateuch is the product of a combination of sources, then it is not really a criticism, but a conclusion. If it is used in its broadest sense, as it often is, to refer to the study of the literary history of any biblical text, then it is not really about sources.

So then what is this book about? It is about the literary history of the Pentateuch, and about the history of that literary history: what theories scholars have put forward, but just as importantly why they have put forward those theories in particular. Some of those theories involve sources; others don't. While my own perspective will become apparent, the aim of this volume is not to make a positive argument for any one position. It is, rather, to recognize that the literature on this topic is vast and complicated, and goes back to the very beginnings of critical biblical inquiry. No scholarly position exists independent of those that preceded it. The study of the literary history of the Pentateuch, like that of the rest of the Bible (but perhaps even more so), has not occurred in a vacuum, but has always been swept up in broader intellectual trends.

The aim of this volume is to lay bare and make accessible to non-specialists the shape of pentateuchal scholarship, to orient them to its history and current trends, and thus to allow them to more clearly understand and evaluate the scholarship, past and present, that has shaped discussions around the formation of the Pentateuch.

As noted above, source criticism (defined narrowly or broadly) didn't begin with a desire to find sources in the biblical text. It began with a problem. The problem was that the Pentateuch didn't seem to make great sense as a narrative. Its overall shape was reasonable enough, but its details—that's where things got tricky. Some stories seem to be told twice: Moses getting water from a rock in the wilderness (Exod 17:1–7 and Num 20), for example, or God changing Jacob's name to Israel (Gen 32:29 and Gen 35:10). Sometimes things are told twice even within a single story: God informing Noah about the flood and telling him to bring animals onto the ark (Gen 6:13–21 and Gen 7:1–4), or God promising not to bring another flood (Gen 8:21–22 and Gen 9:9–17). These repetitions are known as doublets. Then there are those places where one passage seems to disagree with another: contradictions. What is the name of Moses's father-in-law: Reuel (Exod 2:18) or Jethro (Exod 3:1)? Is the Tent of Meeting in the middle of the camp (Num 2–3) or is it outside the camp altogether (Exod 33:7)? Again, such issues arise not only between passages, but even within single episodes. How many animals was Noah to bring onto the ark: two of each species (Gen 6:19–20) or fourteen of some species and two of others (Gen 7:2–3)? How long did the flood last: forty days (Gen 7:12) or 150 days (Gen 7:24)? As these last examples suggest, doublets and contradictions often come together. The same basic event or speech is related twice, but with differences. In Numbers 14, God declares that the entire exodus generation will die in the wilderness, except for Caleb (Num 14:21–24). Then, in a doublet, God declares again that the entire exodus generation will die in the wilderness, except for—in a contradiction—both Caleb and Joshua (Num 14:29–35).

The legal sections of the Pentateuch exhibit the same sorts of issues. Laws are repeated, sometimes nearly verbatim, in multiple places: for example, the somewhat befuddling instruction not to boil a kid in its mother's milk shows up in Exod 23:19, Exod 34:26, and Deut 14:21. A basic topic may show up over and over again, whether it be festival instructions (Exod 23:14–17; Lev 23; Num 28–29; Deut 16), the treatment of enslaved persons (Exod 21:2–10; Lev 25:39–46; Deut 15:12–18), or the establishment of cities of refuge (Num 35 and Deut 19). Doublets—triplets, even—and also contradictions. How is the Passover offering to be prepared: by boiling (Deut 16:7) or by roasting and definitely not by boiling (Exod 12:9)? Is one permitted to slaughter a cow or sheep whenever and wherever one wants (Deut 12:20–21), or is one required to slaughter such animals only as sacrificial offerings at the sanctuary (Lev 17:3–7)?

There are hundreds of such examples that could be brought. And this very abundance of issues changes the nature of the question, from a localized oddity here and there to a more global problem affecting the entirety of the Pentateuch. How this concatenation of doublets, contradictions, and related literary issues is to be explained has varied substantially over the past three centuries—and that variation is the subject of this book. But at the heart of all those variations, of all the theories, is the common underlying set of problems.

Not included in this set of problems, perhaps somewhat surprisingly, is the question of whether or not the Pentateuch was written by Moses. In part this is because the traditional claim of Mosaic authorship had slowly been eroding, quietly and then more openly, for hundreds of years. There were simply too many indications that Moses could not have written parts of the Pentateuch, most famously the narration of his death at the end of Deuteronomy. (My personal favorite of all such passages is Num 12:3, where, according to the traditional position, Moses is supposed to have written about himself, "Now Moses was a very humble man, more so than any other man on earth.") And in part Mosaic authorship is not precisely a source-critical concern because what is at stake is not who wrote the Pentateuch but whether any one hand, Moses's or otherwise, could be responsible for it. As we will see, some early critical scholars sought to maintain both a source-critical understanding of the Pentateuch's origins and, at the same time, something like the traditional claim that Moses wrote—or at least wrote down—the text. In other words, saying that Moses wrote the Pentateuch alleviates none of the literary problems of the Pentateuch—but, at the same time, saying that Moses didn't write the Pentateuch doesn't solve those problems either.

It is one of the main observations of this book that the various theories of the Pentateuch's composition are inseparable from the broader intellectual trends of their times. It is, therefore, worth noting that the same can and should be said for the identification of the literary problems that underlies those theories. What separates modern critical approaches from interpretive positions that preceded them is not the recognition of the literary phenomena in question—the doublets and contradictions—but rather the designation of such as "problems" to be solved. Close reading of the biblical text is hardly a recent trend. Those readers for whom every minute detail of the Bible was worthy of nearly infinite study and speculation, especially the classical Jewish interpreters of the first millennium CE, had long since recognized virtually every potential bump in the Pentateuch: every repetition, every contradiction, every slight variation. They simply didn't see these as problems, but rather as opportunities for a deeper sort of understanding. They brought to their reading a set of assumptions about the biblical text: the belief that it was divinely inspired, to be sure, but also the position that it was endlessly significant. Doublets and contradictions were not only not errors, they were sites for interpretations that sought to make a new sense out of a text understood to be designed for this very interpretive purpose.[1]

It is easy enough, from where we sit, to write off such interpretive assumptions as ancient, or uncritical, or otherwise a mere product of a different era. Yet what we describe as modern and critical interpretations are themselves equally a product of their era, of their time and place. We read the literary phenomena of the Pentateuch as "problems" not because they are so by definition, or in some objective sense. They are problems because we have different assumptions about what texts are, and especially about what the Bible is; because we are interested in a different set of questions. When the rabbis saw a contradiction, they asked, "What meaning can we make from this?" When critical scholars see a contradiction, we ask, "How did the text come to look this way?" Both questions are, in a sense, really asking, "Why is the text like this?"

1. Kugel, *Traditions of the Bible*, 1–30, esp. 14–19.

The Enlightenment brought with it a rejection of traditional and traditionally authoritative truth claims, particularly those handed down by the religious establishment. But the rationalistic perspective that replaced those traditional claims is equally bound to its own set of authorities and establishments. One is not true while the other is false; rather, both operate within their own systems of meaning-making and interpretation, with their own assumptions. Thus we should not declare either the traditional or the critical approach better or worse, preferable or not. Rather, we should recognize that we continue largely to inhabit the post-Enlightenment rationalistic mindset. Source criticism is no more a challenge to traditional interpretive modes than, say, medieval scholasticism is to source criticism.

If the Enlightenment set the terms for source-critical inquiry, subsequent intellectual and cultural trends, in particular German Romanticism, had significant and lasting impact on how that inquiry was carried out. These will be explored in more detail over the course of this book. Along with these trends we can see a set of ongoing discourses within biblical studies that regularly intersect with and influence the question of the Pentateuch's composition, sometimes openly, sometimes only implicitly. Although these too will be treated more fully in the chapters to come, I will set some of them out briefly here.

Underlying virtually every assessment of the Pentateuch's literary history is a claim, almost always unstated, about the nature of the biblical text, and of the sources that constitute it. To put it bluntly: Are or were these texts fundamentally Scripture, or not? When we talk about sources of the Pentateuch, are we talking about mini-Pentateuchs, or proto-Pentateuchs? What sort of status did these literary materials have prior to, or even after, they became part of the Pentateuch as we now have it? Assumptions about textual authority are often transferred—rightly or wrongly, but usually unwittingly—from later understandings of the Bible back onto its earlier manifestations. These assumptions have a significant impact on how one imagines, among other things, the relationship between sources, the potential for them to be altered or updated, and the ways that they communicate.

Related to the question of the nature of the biblical text is that of the relationship between the Bible and historical reality. Can the composition of the biblical material be decisively pegged to a particular historical context? Is the text a window onto the past (even if not the one the text itself describes)? Or is it comprehensible only when read as emerging from a specific time and circumstance? We might see in this one of the primary rationales for source-critical investigations in the first place: not the better understanding of the biblical material, but rather of ancient Israel's cultural, social, and intellectual history. In that light, to what degree do preconceptions about that history retroactively influence the literary analysis? To what extent does how one dates a biblical text affect the way one interprets it, and vice versa? Can the literary analysis be separated from the secondary uses to which it is put?

A recurring concern in biblical studies more generally, but specifically in the study of the Pentateuch, is the potential oral, or pre-literary, origins of the text. Sentiments have waxed and waned dramatically on this topic over the past 150 years. Some scholars have seen the text as almost a written distillation of oral tradition; others have discounted any pre-literary existence for these materials altogether. Pre-literary traditions—and the denial of the same—have been used to explain literary features of the Pentateuch. Where multiple texts overlap in content or theme, is that to be understood as a reflection of a common pre-literary background? Or, barring the possibility of such a background, is such overlap instead proof of direct literary dependence? On the other side of orality is what is commonly now known as scribalism: the role and impact of those literary professionals who were materially responsible for the creation, copying, maintenance, and alteration of written materials. To what extent is the formation of the Pentateuch the result of the work of scribes, and how much does their work overlap with broader cultural forces in ancient Israel?

Perhaps the trickiest issue, both to identify and to talk about, is the way that scholars' faith affects the types of analysis they perform and conclusions that they draw. There is often something of a taboo around even raising this discussion, in part because we consider ourselves to operate within a realm of pure rationalism, good post-Enlightenment scholars that we are. Yet rationalism isn't the same as secularism, and biblical criticism, even in the last two hundred years, is predominantly practiced by scholars who have faith commitments of one kind or another. Whether consciously or not, those religious stances influence the scholars who hold them. Historically, there is some irony in this: many early advocates of source criticism were considered near-heretics by their religious communities. Some were removed from their university chairs or forced to resign from their positions. Yet such unfortunate reactions stem more from the conflict between dogma and rationalistic inquiry than that between faithfulness and faithlessness. As we will see, scholars and scholarship that were treated as anathema by more traditional religious authorities in their time were, in fact, still working quite clearly within the conceptual frameworks of their faith communities. To recognize this is to call sharply into question the identification of Enlightenment thought with objectivity. Scholars are always influenced by who they are and where, intellectually and culturally, they come from; their scholarship is always inflected by their context and background. While the academic study of the Bible has unquestionably moved the needle on how the text and its origins are understood, it is also the case that personal and communal faith commitments have continued to determine the shape of that study. Were the pentateuchal sources scriptural, or authoritative, before they were taken up into the Pentateuch? How were the different stages of the Pentateuch's growth understood by the communities responsible for them? What sort of comprehensibility should, or must, we expect from the redaction of the Pentateuch? What biblical materials are judged to be early or late, and why? What, in the end, is the purpose of inquiring after the text's origins at all?

The history of source criticism is inseparable from the cultural and intellectual contexts in which it has been carried out, from the particular theories offered to the very basic questions that lie at the heart of the scholarship. It is only within those broader frameworks that we can comprehend and evaluate what scholars have to say about the literary history of the text and why they are asking these questions in the first place. Once we recognize this, the history of source criticism becomes relevant, not merely as a curiosity, or for understanding the ideas of the past, but for thinking in the present, and looking ahead to the future. When we come to these same texts, what kinds of questions are we asking, and why? What assumptions do we bring to our reading? What ideas do we share with those that came before us, and which do we leave behind?

1

EARLY THEORIES

Sources, Fragments, Supplements

For roughly a millennium and a half, the fundamental unity, and Mosaic authorship, of the Pentateuch went largely unquestioned. There were, from the Christian church fathers to the medieval Jewish commentators, a few passages here and there that were noted as having been potentially written after Moses, such as the verses about his death and burial in Deuteronomy 34. And it was certainly acknowledged that the text of the Pentateuch, like that of the entire Bible, had probably experienced some corruption, and perhaps even correction and minor expansion, through the process of transmission. Although on the surface of the text one might find a few encrustations, the bulk of the Pentateuch was still understood as a solid block of unified, Mosaic writing.

By the beginning of the eighteenth century, this was no longer the case. The biblical text had of course not changed; it was the assumptions about how that text should be read that were different. The rise of humanism and rationalism in Europe in the fifteenth to seventeenth centuries saw new attempts to read the Bible free from the interpretive, ethical, and theological constraints of established ecclesiastical authority. This was expressed most clearly in the humanist refrain *ad fontes*, "to the sources," which indicated both a resurgent interest in the classical texts of pagan antiquity and a revitalized investigation of the Bible. Of particular interest to these modern scholars were precisely those aspects of the biblical text that had been obscured by the interpretive veils of medieval scholasticism: its original languages and historical contexts. Thus these centuries saw a renewed study of Biblical Hebrew and Greek, along with other philological projects: new translations, critical editions, and polyglot Bibles, all of which expanded knowledge about the biblical text while simultaneously destabilizing it. The firm theological teachings that ecclesiastical scholars derived from the Bible were replaced with inquiries into its origins, the history of its transmission, and the variety of its interpretations across time and space. The Bible was understood no longer as scripture, but rather as text; not in its own category, but to be read alongside, and as part of, the larger corpus of ancient literature.[1]

Despite the humanist and rationalist stances of these eighteenth-century scholars, they were hardly cloistered from the religious worlds in which they lived. This was especially so in the wake of the Reformation, which took the humanist adage *ad fontes* and supplemented it with *sola scriptura*, thus creating a powerful and decidedly confessional rationale for the renewed study of the Bible's origins. The argument worked both ways: Protestant

1. See Legaspi, *Death of Scripture*.

scholars looked to the text to counter the overweening interpretive power of the established church; Catholic scholars took up the Protestant intellectual weapons to fight back with them; and some understood humanist scholarship as a means of finding ground common to both sides. None, however, worked in some sort of cultural vacuum. The Bible was worth investigating not despite its centrality to Christianity and its internal disputations, but because of it.

Traditional Mosaic authorship was one major pillar of accepted tradition to fall in the face of these new inquiries. From a rationalist perspective, the logical problems presented by the Pentateuch could no longer simply be attributed to, dismissed as, or explained by the cryptic communication style of the divine text. What did the rationalists find? An increasingly observed number of anachronisms (that is, references that must postdate Moses); internal contradictions or other oddities; repetitions, both within and between passages; stylistic variation; the simple fact that the text speaks of Moses in the third person throughout. All of these spoke against unqualified Mosaic authorship. Yet scholars were seemingly loathe to abandon any role for Moses altogether in the formation of the text. There were, after all, those passages that describe Moses actually putting things down in writing; references even within the Pentateuch to other, older written sources; and there was the lingering weight of tradition, which had long attributed these books to Moses's hand. Inescapable, it seemed, was an assumption that the biblical narrative was, in essence, true. That is, the very existence of Moses, and his status in Israel's history as law-giver, were not fundamentally in question. The story of the Pentateuch was an important piece of evidence in the investigation into its own origins.

Thus the very scholars who critically identified in the Pentateuch sign upon sign of both post-Mosaic materials and multiple hands in the text posited explanations that could still accommodate some form of Mosaic responsibility. Moses perhaps wrote the parts of the text that he is said to have actually written down—notably the laws—while others composed the rest. Moses perhaps did write something like the Pentateuch, but that original copy was lost, or rearranged, or poorly copied, or some similar material explanation, and was subsequently rewritten, reconstructed, recompiled from its authentic Mosaic version. Moses perhaps did not write parts of the Pentateuch himself, but rather directed others to write down the events of his time, which he then put together and passed down. In their proposals these scholars explored the limits of potential Mosaic involvement in the composition of the Pentateuch. Some parts of the text were ostensibly earlier than Moses; some were seemingly later; some could well be contemporaneous. What was the maximum that could be attributed to Moses given the textual problems? What was the minimum that the Pentateuch required?

Scholars largely agreed on the literary phenomena that demanded explanation: the anachronisms, the contradictions, the repetitions, the stylistic variation. Common to most proposals was a multiplicity of hands and a notion of underlying written sources. Missing, however, was a systematic, thorough-going explanation. Such explanations did emerge, beginning in the middle of the eighteenth century—yet, as we will see, these new broader theories of how the text came to be (sources, fragments, and supplements) would, like their predecessors, walk the line between grappling with the problematic textual phenomena and maintaining the traditional Christian centrality of the Pentateuch.

In 1753, a French Catholic medical doctor, Jean Astruc, published a volume of his *Conjectures* on the composition of Genesis.[2] He knew well the troubling literary phenomena identified by earlier scholars, and to them he added a further oddity: the varied use of divine appellations. Interpreters had certainly long taken note of the fact that some passages refer to Israel's god by a title—"Elohim," or "God"—while other passages use the deity's proper name, "Yahweh," traditionally "translated" as "Lord." Suspecting that the alternation of divine names might be related to the existence of other problems in the text, Astruc took the simple step of dividing Genesis (as well as Exod 1–2) into two main columns: those that use "Elohim," and those that use "Yahweh." Each represented a continuous narrative thread, beginning with creation and moving through the history of Israel's ancestors. Here, for the first time, scattered texts and textual phenomena were aligned into large-scale, independent documents. While previous scholars had been concerned mostly with the deconstruction of the traditionally unified text, Astruc turned to the task of reunification. "It was natural to try to take apart Genesis to separate all the different bits that are confounded there, to reunite those that are of the same kind and that appear to have belonged to the same Memoires."[3] The two resulting narratives, A ("Elohim") and B ("Yahweh"), Astruc believed to be source documents for Israel's early history, collected

2. Astruc, *Conjectures*.

3. Astruc, *Conjectures*, 143 (translation mine).

by Moses and arranged in the very columns that Astruc himself used. Astruc also recognized a handful of passages that fit neatly into neither, dealing mostly with non-Israelite peoples (such as the list of Edomite kings in Gen 36), and gave them their own columns, proposing that they were the product of foreign record-keeping, in the same way that the main columns were for Israel. Astruc's various columns—the documentary sources of Genesis—were mixed together into their present state not by intent, but through the sloppiness of copyists in the generations after Moses.

As an example of Astruc's approach, we might look at his treatment of the beginning of the flood story, in Genesis 6:5—7:5. Following the use of the divine names, Astruc divided the text as follows (*italics* is Astruc's B document ["Yahweh"], and plain text is his A document ["Elohim"]):

> *Yahweh saw that the wickedness of humankind was great in the earth, and that every inclination of the thoughts of their hearts was only evil continually. And Yahweh was sorry that he had made humankind on the earth, and it grieved him to his heart. So Yahweh said, "I will blot out from the earth the human beings I have created—people together with animals and creeping things and birds of the air, for I am sorry that I have made them." But Noah found favor in the sight of Yahweh.* These are the descendants of Noah. Noah was a righteous man, blameless in his generation; Noah walked with God. And Noah had three sons, Shem, Ham, and Japheth. Now the earth was corrupt in God's sight, and the earth was filled with violence. And God saw that the earth was corrupt; for all flesh had corrupted its ways upon the earth. And God said

to Noah, "I have determined to make an end of all flesh, for the earth is filled with violence because of them; now I am going to destroy them along with the earth. Make yourself an ark of cypress wood; make rooms in the ark, and cover it inside and out with pitch. This is how you are to make it: the length of the ark three hundred cubits, its width fifty cubits, and its height thirty cubits. Make a roof for the ark, and finish it to a cubit above; and put the door of the ark in its side; make it with lower, second, and third decks. For my part, I am going to bring a flood of waters on the earth, to destroy from under heaven all flesh in which is the breath of life; everything that is on the earth shall die. But I will establish my covenant with you; and you shall come into the ark, you, your sons, your wife, and your sons' wives with you. And of every living thing, of all flesh, you shall bring two of every kind into the ark, to keep them alive with you; they shall be male and female. Of the birds according to their kinds, and of the animals according to their kinds, of every creeping thing of the ground according to its kind, two of every kind shall come in to you, to keep them alive. Also take with you every kind of food that is eaten, and store it up; and it shall serve as food for you and for them." Noah did this; he did all that God commanded him. *Then Yahweh said to Noah, "Go into the ark, you and all your household, for I have seen that you alone are righteous before me in this generation. Take with you seven pairs of all clean animals, the male and its mate; and a pair of the animals that are not clean, the male and its mate; and seven pairs of the birds of the air also, male and female, to keep their kind alive on the face of all the earth. For in seven days I will send rain on*

> *the earth for forty days and forty nights; and every living thing that I have made I will blot out from the face of the ground." And Noah did all that Yahweh had commanded him.*

The distribution of the divine names is clear and consistent. But what is solved here is not just the alternating divine names, but a slew of other problems as well. The canonical repetition of both God deciding to bring a flood and God's instructions to Noah in anticipation of the flood is now resolved, with each narrative having exactly one of each feature. The contradictions in the story are also alleviated: in one story it is humanity that is evil, while in the other it is all flesh; in one Yahweh instructs Moses to bring seven pairs of clean animals and birds, while in the other God tells Moses to bring two of every kind of animal. Stylistic variation is explained as well: the A story is verbose, with technical details and internal phraseological repetition, while the B story is somewhat more straightforward. Thus, while divine names were the key mechanism for Astruc's analysis, it was the narrative difficulties of the canonical text that are in fact solved by that analysis.

Astruc's work was extended and popularized by the German scholar Johann Gottfried Eichhorn, often recognized as the founder of modern biblical criticism. Eichhorn accepted Astruc's main insight and deepened the analysis, making even clearer how the division of Genesis according to the divine names helped to solve many of the commonly identified narrative inconsistencies. It was in regard to Eichhorn's work that the phrase "documentary hypothesis" began to be used.

In this early documentary theory we can see an extension of the same balancing act recognizable in earlier scholarly proposals. There are textual issues to be resolved, but there is also the basic reliability of the biblical narrative itself to be contended with. Thus, multiple sources—but sources collected by Moses. Somewhat remarkably, these sources were not, themselves, originally scriptural. Some of them, in fact, were downright pagan, borrowed from the nations that Moses encountered on his travels, such as the Midianites. What imprints them with the status of scripture, then, is not their origins, but their having been taken up by Moses, their inclusion in the eventual Pentateuch. This is not quite Mosaic authorship, but it is still Mosaic responsibility, for the text of Genesis at least.

The fact that Astruc and Eichhorn separated Genesis (and Exod 1–2) from the remainder of the Pentateuch is also part of this same negotiation between critical and traditional stances toward the Bible. Genesis was treated apart not because the two different divine names cease to be a factor after Exod 2—though this is, ironically, true. Rather, Astruc and Eichhorn assumed that once the story reached the time of Moses's adult life Moses wouldn't have needed external written sources. (Astruc understood the narrative of Exod 1–2, Moses's childhood, to have been written by Moses's father.) The underlying question here was one of anachronism: how did Moses write the history of what happened before he was born? This question, notably, assumes the basic trustworthiness of the biblical narrative.

Indeed, Astruc's analysis was meant not to undermine traditional views of the Pentateuch, but rather to reinforce them, even while accepting some of the challenges of previous scholarship. "Moses is completely acquitted of all the errors of carelessness and inattention which even the most guarded commentators have laid at his door; while the reverence and faith he deserves as the wisest of law-givers and one of the greatest prophets whom God has raised up is increased; and at the same time the trust which he deserves as the clearest, the most exact and the most truthful of historians must be multiplied."[4] So too Eichhorn:

> The credibility of the book [i.e., Genesis] obviously gains by it. . . . The historian is no longer obliged to rely on one reporter in the history of the most distant past; and in the duplicated narratives of the same event he is not obliged to force into harmony the unessential differences in accessory circumstances by artificial devices. He sees in such divergences the marks of independent origin, and finds in their agreement the main important mutual confirmation. . . . The world will cease to lay on Moses the burden of the sins of his younger expositors.[5]

In the late eighteenth century, an English priest named Alexander Geddes looked past Genesis to the rest of the Pentateuch.[6] Eichhorn had already suggested that these books comprised a collection of once-independent materials, though he continued to attribute them to Moses. Geddes was more doubtful: some of the materials might have been Mosaic, or pre-Mosaic, but the collecting of them he dated more probably to the time of Solomon. He also claimed, not without merit, that what was true of the last four books was likely true also of the first. He viewed Genesis as a collection of fragments, rather than as derived from two continuous source documents.

4. Astruc, *Conjectures*, 491. Translation in Smend, *From Astruc to Zimmerli*, 10–11.

5. Quoted in Carpenter and Harford-Battersby, *Hexateuch*, 70.

6. Geddes, *Holy Bible*.

Anticipating a later interest in pre-literary origins, Geddes traced much of the material in Genesis back to oral tradition: "Some remarkable tree under which a patriarch had resided; some pillar which he had erected; some ford which he had crossed; some spot where he had encamped; some field which he had purchased; the tomb in which he had been laid—all these served as so many links to hand his story down to posterity."[7]

In the first decade of the nineteenth century, the German scholar Johann Vater brought the ideas of Geddes to full fruition.[8] Many of the standard criteria for discerning different hands in the Pentateuch continued to be relevant for Vater. Repetitions and contradictions, style and tone, were duly noted, as were different names, for the deity as well as for the mountain in the wilderness (Horeb in Deuteronomy, Sinai in the preceding books). To these Vater, like Geddes ahead of his time, added more formal literary considerations. A number of passages are marked off from their surroundings by the use of introductory or concluding phrases: "These are the generations of," ten times in Genesis; "These are the statutes and ordinances and laws that Yahweh established between himself and the people of Israel on Mount Sinai through Moses," at the end of Lev 26 and similarly at the end of Lev 27. Seemingly self-contained stories were just that: the story of Cain and Abel in Gen 4 had, in Vater's view, no connection with what preceded or followed it. Similarly, the long list of tribal gifts for the tabernacle in Num 7 was once independent, as was the wilderness itinerary of Num 33. Some units were themselves composite: Vater recognized the same basic two threads in

7. Geddes, *Holy Bible*, xix.

8. Vater, *Commentar*.

the opening of the flood narrative as in Astruc's analysis, and on the same grounds. But other passages that had similar internal difficulties, like the plagues cycle of Exod 7–11, he took as a single segment.

Where Vater departed from Astruc and Eichhorn was not in the recognition that different parts of Genesis, in particular, used varying designations for the deity, but rather in the question of whether all of the passages that used Elohim or Yahweh belonged together in a single continuous whole. His position was fundamentally skeptical:

> In general, it is a very daring undertaking to show for books that developed from individual documents not only that they are indeed made up of individual documents, but also how many they are made up of, and even to which of these documents every word of Genesis belongs. . . . But it would be even more striking if a device as simple as the difference in the names of God in Genesis, almost entirely by itself, sufficed to determine most precisely where each of the individual pieces began and ended, as well as to reassemble from all the torn-apart pieces the original whole in which those pieces are once said to have been united.[9]

Though, as with Geddes, Vater nominally retained the possibility of Mosaic authorship of some parts of the Pentateuch, he minimized Moses's involvement to practically nothing. Rather, he was insistent, in line with what are now recognized as basic critical claims, that the pentateuchal materials reflect not the era they describe, but a later era in which they were written. (His understanding of those later periods of Israel's history, somewhat ironically, were based on a fundamentally uncritical reading

9. Vater, *Commentar*, 713, 715 (translation mine).

of history of Israel presented in the Bible itself. As we will see, this is a not uncommon tendency in scholarship.) In this Vater took the earlier scholarly recognition of pentateuchal anachronisms, once used to pick out a few passages here and there that might not be from Moses, and extrapolated it over the entire text. Each of the individual fragments that make up the Pentateuch, now that Moses was no longer assumed as author, could be investigated for its compositional context.

At the same time, Vater admitted that there was plenty of material in the Pentateuch that likely had a long history of development, going back to oral tradition. As a result, firmly dating the origins of any fragments, or even the whole, he considered impossible. The etiologies of Genesis—the names of people, places, altars, trees, etc.—were signs of the persistence of traditional knowledge. The extraordinary, even supernatural, aspects of the text (such as the ages found in the genealogies of Gen 5, or the Israelites' clothing not wearing out in the wilderness), along with the evident contradictions between various passages, were indications of the vagaries of the material's transmission over the centuries. In this way Vater maintained the basic historicity of the Pentateuch, even while removing its traditional author. Mosaic authorship, he argued, was questionable; Moses, as historical figure, was not.

Vater opened his investigation into the composition of the Pentateuch by articulating the rationale for it:

> Ancient messages lie before us in the Pentateuch. It is not just this great age that makes them important to us; they also have wide-ranging interest because of their content and because of the spirit of piety and religiosity that prevails only in the writings of this nation

> [Israel]. A closer examination of the condition of these books is fully worthy of our attention. From this alone can a definite judgment be made as to the age, origin, and value of these books, and of the age, origin, and value of the information contained in them.[10]

Notably, Vater here sets aside the traditional view that the Pentateuch is of central importance because it is the divinely inspired word of God—or of Moses. Anticipating his conclusions regarding Mosaic authorship, Vater relocates the essence of the Pentateuch from heaven to earth: from the deity to the spirit of the Israelite people. In this we can recognize an early reflex of German Romanticism, particularly as expressed in the work of Johann Gottfried Herder, with its appeal to the people, the *Volk*, as the origin of culture, past and present.

Twenty years after Vater put forward his fragmentary model, the German scholar Heinrich Ewald published an extensive rebuttal, focusing particularly on Genesis.[11] Ewald reaffirmed a traditional unitary model for Genesis, not by simply returning to pre-critical approaches, but by bringing in comparative and ethnographic material from the Near East. Variation in names, lack of interest in perfect internal consistency, the tendency to jump from one story to another—all these he attributed to the narrative style of "the Orient." Ewald's work, despite its basically conservative stance, marks another new step in the study of the Pentateuch's origins. Now comparative study, not just historical but of literary style, was relevant.

10. Vater, *Commentar*, 393.

11. Ewald, *Komposition der Genesis*.

Ewald, however, soon altered his views on the nature of the Pentateuch. Less than a decade later, he outlined a new model, in which the main story of the Pentateuch, running from creation through the death of Moses and on into the conquest of Canaan in the book of Joshua, was due to a single author.[12] That author, however, had taken up into his work even older writings, including the Decalogue and the Covenant Code. At a later time, a second version of Israel's history was produced (itself also based on ancient material, such as the wars of Abraham in Gen 14). This second version, Ewald posited, differed in style—and, in Genesis at least, in its use of the divine name. An editor then combined these two versions, using the first as the basis for the whole, and interlacing the second as a supplement. Ewald thus laid out, in only a few paragraphs, a model that would, with some variation, eventually play a major part in pentateuchal criticism: a scattering of older written texts, taken up and framed by a comprehensive narrative, which itself was subsequently supplemented by a later hand.

Although Ewald moved significantly away from his earlier view of the Pentateuch as the work of a single author, he did so without abandoning his sense of it as still fundamentally a unity. "The unity of the book must still be asserted, the progress of the narrative being complete; duplicate or contradictory stories about the same event are nowhere to be found, at least according to the sense of the last author."[13] With this construction Ewald rescued the final form of the Pentateuch from the notion, growing over the prior few centuries, that it was largely haphazard: from Vater's barely coordinated collection of loose

12. Ewald, review of Stähelin.

13. Ewald, review of Stähelin, 604 (translation mine).

fragments back to Astruc's sloppy scribal confounding of early documents all the way to Spinoza's various materials "very promiscuously collected and heaped together."[14] Ewald, by insisting on the idea of a "last author," found meaning, even purpose, in the combination of all the constituent parts of the Pentateuch, and thus in the whole.

Ewald would eventually provide a fuller picture of his theory, and though the precise details are too complicated to present here we may note a few salient features.[15] The earliest texts in the Pentateuch are identifiable by their archaic style, often poetic, and by their "purely historical" nature: the Song of the Sea in Exod 15, for example, or the brief songs of Num 21:14 and 27, taken from an older collection, the "Book of the Wars of Yahweh." Ewald also posited the existence, now only in fragments, of a biography of Moses that must have been written soon after his life. He posited a "Book of Covenants" that brought together the biography of Moses with traditions about covenants made by the patriarchs and between Israel and God in Exod 24. This work also included the Decalogue, which already existed independently. These early written sources both reinforce and presume the history related in the Pentateuch. They form the backbone for the overarching narrative. Even in these early pieces we can already see Ewald working with a supplementary approach, in which a later author brings together and organizes preexisting independent works under a coherent conceptual framework.

For Ewald, three major narrative works form the bulk of Genesis–Numbers, each independent of the others but attributable to successive historical periods. The "Book

14. Spinoza, *Treatise*, 135.

15. Ewald, *Geschichte*, 1:94–193.

of Origins," dated to the tenth-century reigns of David or Solomon, was the name given to the first thoroughgoing pentateuchal narrative, beginning with Gen 1 and continuing through the primeval history, patriarchs, life of Moses, and conquest of the land, including the building of the tabernacle and some of the ritual legislation of Leviticus. A similarly substantial history emerged from the northern kingdom of Israel in the generations after Solomon, including most of the Joseph story (Gen 37–47). Roughly a century later another author, influenced by early Israelite prophecy and focused on issues related to sin (e.g., Gen 3), created yet another narrative, particularly notable for its beautifully descriptive style.

These various works would be interwoven by a still later author, who added a few passages of his own but was primarily concerned to bring together the various extant histories. In Ewald's view, this was a product of its time: the abundance of available written records, and the increasing learnedness of the masses, led to a need for clarity. With this stage, the first four books of the Pentateuch (plus the book of Joshua) were created. The final steps were the writing of Deuteronomy—an independent text but a conscious reworking of the earlier materials, updating them for the context of the seventh century—and the combination of Deuteronomy with the rest of the Pentateuch.

Though Ewald's ideas have come to be known as the "supplementary" model, what he proposed was really something of a hybrid. There were fragments that had been gathered together; there were longer documents that had been combined. What Ewald found in the growth of the Pentateuch that his predecessors had not was intention. Fragments were gathered together, but were overlaid with broad ideological frameworks. Longer documents were combined, but with one as the base and the others as expansions. While independent works may have had their own ideas and existence, whenever the major parts of the Pentateuch were assembled—the "Book of Origins," the bulk of Genesis–Numbers, and, with the inclusion of Deuteronomy, the whole—it was done on purpose and with a purpose.

This sense of intentionality cannot be separated from the other major new feature of Ewald's approach: the introduction of evolutionary development into the reconstruction of the Pentateuch's literary history. This can be seen in multiple aspects of Ewald's model. In terms of the assumed purpose of the texts, Ewald granted to the earliest fragments a "purely historical" intention, while subsequent writings had broader agendas, whether ritual or prophetic or political. Notably, virtually all of Ewald's earliest fragments dealt with the interaction of Israel with foreign peoples. (This included even the extant fragments of his purported Moses biography, which consisted entirely of his interactions with Jethro.) The historical trustworthiness of the texts therefore also decreased over time: the biography of Moses was probably accurate, while Deuteronomy was freely retelling earlier materials. There was evolution also in the development of Israelite literature: early texts were short, archaic, poetic; longer texts were a later phenomenon.

Each identifiable text was, for Ewald, representative of a stage in the development of Israelite thought, from simple to complex, from historical to theological. Moreover, these stages could be roughly and relatively dated, each one pegged to a period of the history of Israel as described in the Bible. The earliest fragments were from the period described in the Pentateuch; later writings were aligned with successive eras from Judges through 2 Kings. The Pentateuch is, in this sense, both witness to and confirmation of the essential historicity of the Bible. At each stage, the spirit of the Israelite people could be seen, growing and developing.

Sources, fragments, and supplements—despite the clear differences between these three early approaches, there are also commonalities. The paradox that marks all of these early approaches is the simultaneous maintenance of belief—in the continued authority, even sacrality, of these texts; in the essential historicity of the biblical narrative, including that of the Pentateuch; in the importance of Moses—and respect for the literary evidence that challenges those beliefs. All are responses to the same literary phenomena: the contradictions, doublets, and inconsistencies in the Pentateuch. It is these literary phenomena, more than the question of whether Moses wrote the text, that drive the analyses, and it is in this respect that these scholars moved decisively past the first generations of humanist critics.

Yet, overtly or not, the specter of Moses still hangs over these reconstructions. Each is, in its own way, a struggle against the loss of Mosaic authorship. For centuries, it was the name and authority of Moses that established the historical and theological centrality of the Pentateuch. If Moses was not in fact the author, as had become increasingly clear since the seventeenth century, where was the authority of the Pentateuch to be located? For Astruc and Eichhorn, the authority still belonged to Moses, even if he wasn't properly the author (of Genesis, at least). For Geddes and Vater, it was to be found in the people, the *Volk*, and the traditions that they transmitted down through the generations. For Ewald, the authority of the Pentateuch came from its reflection and verification of the history of Israel as described in the Bible itself.

From another perspective: each of these approaches, while dealing with the loss of traditional Mosaic authorship, locates the determinative moment of meaning-making in a different stage of the Pentateuch's formation. For the early source advocates, it remained with Moses, though as collector more than as author. From the fragmentary perspective, it was in the pieces that were eventually brought together. From the supplementary side, it was in the shaping and reframing of the preexisting materials. The moments are different; the need to find such a moment, however, is the same.

In these three models the ground was prepared for virtually every subsequent development in the field. For every approach to the literary history of the Pentateuch we can ask the same questions:

- Where, or where in the process of textual composition, is authority located?
- To what degree does the textual evidence inform historical reconstruction, or vice versa?
- What is the relationship of oral tradition to written text?
- Does the meaning that one derives from the text change when it is severed from its traditional authorship?

CASE STUDY. GENESIS 28:10–22 (ASTRUC)

In each chapter, we will look at a text—the episode of Jacob's encounter with the divine beings at Bethel—to illustrate how different source-critical theories affect the analysis of a specific passage. We begin here with the analysis of Astruc, who considered the entire passage to belong to a single author, his "B" (or "Yahweh") source.

> [10]Jacob left Beersheba and went toward Haran.
> [11]He came to a certain place and stayed there
> for the night, because the sun had set. Taking
> one of the stones of the place, he put it under
> his head and lay down in that place. [12]And he
> dreamed that there was a stairway set up on the
> earth, the top of it reaching to heaven, and the
> angels of God were ascending and descending
> on it. [13]And Yahweh stood beside him and said,
> "I am Yahweh, the God of Abraham your father
> and the God of Isaac; the land on which you lie
> I will give to you and to your offspring, [14]and
> your offspring shall be like the dust of the earth,
> and you shall spread abroad to the west and to
> the east and to the north and to the south, and
> all the families of the earth shall be blessed in
> you and in your offspring. [15]Know that I am
> with you and will keep you wherever you go
> and will bring you back to this land, for I will
> not leave you until I have done what I have
> promised you." [16]Then Jacob woke from his
> sleep and said, "Surely Yahweh is in this place—
> and I did not know it!" [17]And he was afraid and
> said, "How awesome is this place! This is none
> other than the house of God, and this is the gate
> of heaven." [18]So Jacob rose early in the morning,
> and he took the stone that he had put under his
> head and set it up for a pillar and poured oil on
> the top of it. [19]He called that place Bethel, but

> the name of the city was Luz at the first. 20Then
> Jacob made a vow, saying, "If God will be with
> me and will keep me in this way that I go and
> will give me bread to eat and clothing to wear,
> 21so that I come again to my father's house in
> peace, then Yahweh shall be my god, 22and this
> stone, which I have set up for a pillar, shall be
> God's house, and of all that you give me I will
> surely give one-tenth to you."

Astruc's rationale for assigning this passage to his "B" source is reasonably clear. In 28:13, we find "Yahweh" used both in the narration ("Yahweh stood beside him") and in direct speech ("I am Yahweh"). At the same time, Astruc himself recognized that this episode also contains a number of occurrences of the title "Elohim": "the angels of God" in 28:12, "the house of God" in 28:17 and 22, and "if God will be with me" in 28:20. It is useful to note that Astruc, though famous for separating the text according to the Yahweh/Elohim distinction, was not so mechanical about it. Here he allowed "Elohim" to remain in his "Yahweh" source, suggesting that "house of God" was necessary for the wordplay with Bethel, and that the other uses of "Elohim" were, simply, "exceptions to the rule."[16]

We may also, however, see here how Astruc's effort to divide Genesis into two main strands does not solve every literary issue in the text. Here, for example, he has Jacob's journey to Haran in his "B" source—but he has Isaac's instructions to Jacob to go to Paddan-Aram (not Haran) from Gen 28:2, and Jacob's actual journey to Paddan-Aram in 28:5, as part of the same source. (This may indicate where Astruc drew his lines in terms of what required solving.) Somewhat more difficult is the direct reference back to this story in Gen 35:1—"God said to

16. Astruc, *Conjectures*, 429.

Jacob, 'Arise, go up to Bethel, and settle there. Make an altar to the god who appeared to you when you fled from your brother Esau.'" Astruc assigns this to his "A" source. One can see why: "God said," that is, Elohim, rather than "Yahweh said." Thus although the division of the text according to the divine names was intended to solve the internal contradictions of the canonical text, following that rule too strictly also created some problems.

Astruc is an easy place to start with our case study text, as he leaves it entirely intact. As we will see, few others would do the same.

GUIDING QUESTIONS

1. What sorts of evidence were brought to make the early case for multiple hands in the Pentateuch?
2. What are the essential characteristics of the three main scholarly theories (sources, fragments, and supplements) regarding the literary history of the Pentateuch?
3. How do the theories described in this chapter relate to the earlier tradition of Mosaic authorship?

2

DEFINING THE SOURCES

THOUGH THE FRAGMENTARY AND supplementary models would eventually rise to prominence, scholarship of the mid-nineteenth through mid-twentieth centuries was dominated by the documentary hypothesis. This chapter and the next two will discuss the processes through which this model was solidified, popularized, and complicated. Here we will focus on the documents themselves, for it was in the early to mid-nineteenth century that scholarship began to reach broad agreement on their shape. On what grounds were they identified? What characteristics —literary, ideological, or otherwise—were ascribed to them? How, if at all, were they related to each other? To what extent were they tied to particular historical periods, and why? The assumptions that scholars brought to the project of defining the pentateuchal sources are just as important as the conclusions that they reached.

In 1805, Wilhelm Martin Leberecht de Wette published his short dissertation, a work that would, despite its brevity (under twenty pages), come to stand as one of the most important contributions to the study of the Pentateuch's composition. Its title provides a clear précis of its thesis: "Critical and exegetical dissertation wherein it is shown that Deuteronomy is a work different from the earlier books of the Pentateuch and by a different author, of a more recent age."[1] De Wette understood the books of Genesis–Numbers in line with both Astruc/Eichhorn and Geddes/Vater: Genesis was the product of a combination of two main sources, while Exodus–Numbers was a collection of assorted fragments.[2] Deuteronomy, however, he recognized as its own beast, as it were: both dependent on and independent from the rest of the Pentateuch.

Though de Wette strenuously refused any notion of Mosaic authorship for Genesis–Numbers, he did describe it as a "Mosaic history," and he referred to "the person who compiled the preceding books."[3] Despite the multi-authored nature of the first four books, then, he effectively treated them as a unit, and one that is in all aspects distinguishable from Deuteronomy. Deuteronomy, with both new laws and repetitions of preceding material, represents a sudden and new beginning, entirely unanticipated by the foregoing books. If Deuteronomy had been written to stand as a continuation of the pentateuchal narrative, de Wette argued, there would be no

1. All translations of de Wette's work are taken from Harvey and Halpern, "W. M. L. de Wette's '*Dissertatio Critica. . . .*'" Page numbers in the following citations refer to this translation.

2. De Wette in fact concluded that Exodus–Numbers were fragmentary independently of Vater, whose work he read only once his own was in press (85).

3. Harvey and Halpern, "de Wette's '*Dissertatio Critica . . . ,*'" 74.

need to repeat the story, as happens in detail in Deut 1–3, for example. Rather, it was written as a corrective replacement for the "Mosaic history."

It is on the distinctive style of Deuteronomy, however, that de Wette focused his energy. Central to de Wette's claim, and to the many examples that he brings to support it, is the idea that there is a natural progression of literary expression, from the "spare" and "unsophisticated" style of the first four books to the "expansive" and "prolix" language of Deuteronomy. This sort of evolutionary mindset we have seen already with Ewald (though de Wette preceded Ewald), and will see again, in a variety of manifestations, throughout the history of pentateuchal literary criticism. Also observable in de Wette's treatment of Deuteronomy's style is a common tension between earlier and later materials in the Bible. The earlier texts are "unsophisticated," but are at the same time more honest in their concision. The later texts may be more sophisticated rhetorically, but it is clear that de Wette bore no love for "how flaccid and discursive is the diction."[4] At the heart of de Wette's argument is a Romantic notion of early biblical texts, despite or perhaps precisely because of their literary naiveté, as more closely reflecting authentic Israelite expression. This, too, would come to be a standard element of biblical criticism in the first half of the nineteenth century and beyond.

What de Wette saw in the literary style he saw also in the content of Deuteronomy.

> What the preceding books contain as simple, natural, and unsophisticated, our book presents as embellished, more refined, and corrupted. The mythology we encounter in those

4. Harvey and Halpern, "de Wette's *'Dissertatio Critica . . . ,'*" 77.

> books is uncomplicated and retains the character of what was transmitted by the ancestors; our book presents that mythology moderated by a type of mysticism and a cold, refined, superstitious doctrine. It strives to contrive more refined doctrines, with the primary aim of exalting, in a superstitious fashion, the superiority of the Israelite people.[5]

Again we may recognize the value-laden evolutionary model here, from "natural" to "corrupted"—and, what's more, from "mythology" to "doctrine" and "superstition." These are loaded terms. "Mythology" recalls the exalted Greco-Roman tradition; "doctrine" and "superstition" are often associated, by Protestants, with Catholicism, though de Wette (like Wellhausen after him; see the following chapter) took aim at an easier target: "that doctrine is of the sort that appears to approximate, in a certain fashion later, rabbinical doctrine."[6] The course of biblical history is, for de Wette and many others, one of descent from the "natural" to the abased legalistic doctrine of Judaism, a course that is corrected by Christianity's rejection of precisely that legalistic doctrine.

It may be surprising that de Wette described Deuteronomy in these terms, but not Leviticus, with its mass of cultic regulations and exaltation of the priesthood. Yet here again de Wette relied on style to mark the development of Israelite thought: "We hear in the preceding books the authors promulgating, as if lawyers, so to speak, the laws themselves with simplicity and rigor. Our book seemingly acts contrary to the role of the preacher or teacher

5. Harvey and Halpern, "de Wette's '*Dissertatio Critica . . .*,'" 80.

6. Harvey and Halpern, "de Wette's '*Dissertatio Critica . . .*,'" 80.

of morality."[7] Again simplicity is a virtue—indeed, it is associated with proper moral instruction. It is tempting to hear in this echoes of Martin Luther, who similarly appeals to a conjunction of simplicity and morality. The laws of Leviticus, despite their great detail, still pertain exclusively to the sacrificial practices that, in de Wette's view, are of great antiquity in Israel. Those of Deuteronomy make a more comprehensive claim on the daily life of the Israelite, and may thus be judged to be later.

De Wette's analysis was perhaps most impactful, however, in his treatment of Deuteronomy's law regarding cultic centralization. He observed that almost nowhere in the first four books is there any mention of a singular location for the sanctuary. "History clearly shows that there was a time when the Hebrews were wont to erect altars to offer sacrifices to their God, wherever it was pleasing—as was the custom of the Homeric Greeks."[8] We may note in this statement the appeal to history—though in fact the only "history" that could be said to describe the sacrificial customs of early Israel is that presented in the biblical narrative itself, to which de Wette turned for his proofs. (We may also recognize again the equating of early Israel with classical Greek culture.) The crucial moment in de Wette's argument comes when he aligns the distinct texts treating Israelite sacrificial practice with the progression of Israelite history. "That the various laws of the Pentateuch reflect different periods of time can be demonstrated from this doctrine of the place of sacrifice."[9] The earliest stage is that of Exod 20:24–26, which looks like Homer; the next is that of Lev 17, with

7. Harvey and Halpern, "de Wette's '*Dissertatio Critica* . . . ,'" 80.

8. Harvey and Halpern, "de Wette's '*Dissertatio Critica* . . . ,'" 82.

9. Harvey and Halpern, "de Wette's '*Dissertatio Critica* . . . ,'" 81.

its restriction of sacrifice to the tent of meeting; and the last is that of Deuteronomy, which must, according to de Wette, come from a time when "making sacrifices on the high places was considered sacrilegious."[10]

It is in the context of this discussion that de Wette wrote, merely as a parenthetical aside in a footnote, one of the most momentous sentences in the history of biblical studies: "That the code of laws found by the priest Hilkia was our Deuteronomy one may conclude by a far from improbable conjecture."[11] Without even demonstrating the point, de Wette here laid the groundwork for the longstanding scholarly belief that Deuteronomy was the "book of the Torah" discovered in the reign of Josiah (see 2 Kgs 22–23) and used as the basis for his cultic reforms (mostly focused on centralization of worship in Jerusalem)—and, though de Wette himself did not go so far, for the argument that Deuteronomy was in fact composed at the time of Josiah as well. More than anyone previously, de Wette made the argument that biblical texts can be chronologically ordered in line with their evolutionary development, in terms of both style and content, and that that development can be tracked alongside the history of Israel.

De Wette gave us the first and most significant (and perhaps briefest!) argument for the independence of Deuteronomy, or the source that would come to be known as "D." His grounds for doing so were multiple: form (the seeming new beginning in Deut 1 after the ostensible conclusion at the end of Numbers), style (the verbosity of Deuteronomy), and content (the novel law of centralization). Pervading all of them, however, was a Romantic

10. Harvey and Halpern, "de Wette's '*Dissertatio Critica* . . . ,'" 82.

11. Harvey and Halpern, "de Wette's '*Dissertatio Critica* . . . ,'" 82.

notion of a natural early expression, be it literary or religious, and a later degradation thereof. De Wette observed the ways that Deuteronomy differed from the rest of the Pentateuch, but he didn't stop there. It was not only difference, but development, just as his title indicated: "a work different from the earlier books of the Pentateuch and by a different author"—and, further, "of a more recent age." The literary study of Deuteronomy's compositional distinctiveness is tied to historical reconstruction. And the history that is reconstructed through the literary analysis is, unsurprisingly, the narrative of the Bible itself: from a "natural" worship of Israel's deity "wherever it was pleasing" to centralized worship in Jerusalem.

Half a century later, another German scholar, Hermann Hupfeld, published his analysis of Genesis.[12] As we have seen, since the time of Astruc scholars, like de Wette, had largely assumed that Genesis was mainly composed of two strands: the "Yahweh" source (the "Yahwist"), and the "Elohim" source (the "Elohist"). The precise relationship between the two was a matter of ongoing discussion, but the separation based on the use of the divine names was widely accepted. Though a couple of scholars—including, in fact, de Wette—had suggested that there might be something slightly more complicated going on, it was not until Hupfeld that the next major step in the analysis of Genesis, and the Pentateuch, took hold in scholarship. The basic insight was a simple one: that the division according to the divine names may have resolved many of the inconsistencies in Genesis, but not all of them. The Elohist, in particular, was still full of repetitions and contradictions.

12. Hupfeld, *Quellen*.

As an example, Hupfeld offered the two stories of Jacob naming the site of Bethel.[13] In Gen 35:15, after the deity changes his name from Jacob to Israel, we are told "Jacob called the place where God had spoken with him Bethel." Yet back in Gen 28:19, in the famous episode of "Jacob's ladder," we are told that Jacob, waking from his dream vision, "called that place Bethel." Both stories recount the same event—one that, logically, could hardly have happened twice—but set it at different points in Jacob's life and describe it quite differently. Both, however, refer to the deity as "Elohim," and thus (until Hupfeld) had been ascribed to the same source. In essence, Hupfeld recognized that while the divine names might have been a useful tool for differentiating sources, the divine names themselves did not constitute the problem to be solved. The problem, as had always been the case, was the internal narrative inconsistencies. Hupfeld shifted focus from the divine names back to the content of the narrative—to the simple logic of the story, as with the naming of Bethel.

With this seemingly simple realization, Hupfeld made two significant leaps in the study of the sources. First, and most famously, what was once understood to be a single source in Genesis, the "Elohist" of Astruc, was seen to in fact be two: what Hupfeld termed the "older" and "younger" Elohists. The former would, in time, come to be known as the Priestly document, or "P"; the latter would retain the name "Elohist," and be designated as "E" (and so I will refer to them going forward, for the sake of ease). Both were distinguishable from the Yahwist (or, in its German spelling, "Jahwist"—hence its coming to be known simply as "J"). The use of the divine name was still a factor, but it was not one of mere stylistic choice.

13. Hupfeld, *Quellen*, 38–40.

Just as P and E were separable by their incompatible narrative claims (how many times could Jacob name the same place Bethel?), so too the use of the divine name (or not) in Genesis was a narrative issue. It was not that P and E merely preferred to use the title "Elohim"—it was, rather, that they held the historical opinion that the proper name "Yahweh" was not known to anyone in the patriarchal period (see Exod 6:2). For J, by contrast, humans had been using Yahweh's proper name almost since the beginning of time (see Gen 4:26).

The second major step in Hupfeld's analysis had to do with the literary relationship between the sources. Though they often tell the same stories—as with the naming of Bethel—they do so in disparate and, crucially, in internally coherent ways. That is, each builds its own story-world, independently of the others. For Hupfeld, this meant that none was a mere supplement to another—for why, in such a case, would the later text feel the need to repeat simple facts, or create such blatant contradictions? Who, for instance, knowing that in the base text (what we now call P) the divine name is not revealed to Israel until the time of Moses, would use it willy-nilly throughout the patriarchal, and even primeval, period? Or, vice versa: who, knowing that people had referred to Yahweh by name from time immemorial, could possibly claim that they hadn't known the deity's name until Egypt? Thus Hupfeld offered the clearest arguments not only for P, E, and J, but also for their existence as independent documents.

And yet the canonical text is full of repetitions and blatant contradictions. So Hupfeld needed, more than anyone before him, to give an account of the redaction of the documents into the combined whole. He laid out three basic principles. First, the redactor treated his sources with "loyalty and piety."[14] The documents were, for the redactor, authoritative, and were thus to be preserved as completely as possible wherever possible. This accounts for the repetitions and the contradictions, and also for the observation that, "even after long interruptions and insertions, he does not forget to add the most inconspicuous saved part of the relevant document to the appropriate place."[15] The second principle was that the redactor, despite wanting to preserve as much as possible of his sources, was also intent on creating a single, chronological and (relatively) logical narrative. This required some necessary adjustments: the occasional relocation of an episode from its place in its original document in order to match the overall chronology of the combined story, for instance; or the systematic changing of "Sarah" and "Abraham" to "Sarai" and "Abram" everywhere before Gen 17, even though J and E never knew those characters by those "earlier" names. And the third principle was a reflex of the basic observation regarding the independence of the documents from each other: the redactor must have been a separate figure, later than any of the sources with which he worked. P, E, or J could not have brought the sources together, for they would have been introducing contradiction to their own narrative claims. The redaction could have been accomplished only by someone who knew and respected equally all three sources.

In his arguments regarding the separation of E from P, the relationship among the sources, and the role of the redactor, Hupfeld moved the discussion firmly into the realm of the literary. It was the narrative—the story, the

14. Hupfeld, *Quellen*, 196 (translation mine).

15. Hupfeld, *Quellen*, 198.

plot—that stood at the center of both the problem of the Pentateuch and its solution.

Hupfeld saw himself as advocating for a purely critical analysis of the Pentateuch in the face of two distinct but related forces. In the wake of Astruc and the identification of sources, there was a wave of anti-critical works rejecting the literary-historical approach wholesale. These were easily enough dismissed as confessional bias. Yet Hupfeld was more concerned with a second group: scholars, like early Ewald, who allowed for the existence of multiple authors but were still intent on maintaining a basic unity in the text, a unity that obscured the very narrative distinctions on which Hupfeld grounded his work. We may recall Ewald's claim that "duplicate or contradictory stories about the same event are nowhere to be found, at least according to the sense of the last author." For Hupfeld, such stories were everywhere to be found, and in fact their very presence was what gave definition to the "last author"—that is, the redactor. Without saying so explicitly, Hupfeld offered his analysis as a challenge to the notion that the Pentateuch, even as a multi-authored text, must have a single "meaning." In this he stood in opposition to Ewald's early ideas and anticipated his later ones: he explicitly rejected the supplementary approach.

Where Hupfeld stood in agreement with his predecessors (and contemporaries, and successors), however, was in his understanding of the historical relationship between the sources. As we have seen, he referred to P and E as the "older" and "younger" Elohists. He further claimed that J was younger still. His grounds for doing so should be familiar. P's narrative is simple: it "mainly traces the moments of legal history, but is otherwise short and vague";[16] J's, by contrast, is fuller, more embellished with detail and characterization. This is the same Romantic notion of cultural and literary development we saw in de Wette and Ewald. E stood between P and J chronologically because, for Hupfeld, it stood between them in literary characteristics as well: not as simple as P, not quite as developed as J—"though much nearer to the latter than to the former."[17] In this manner, though unintentionally, Hupfeld successfully dislocated E from P but simultaneously aligned it with J, if not in its composition then in its basic literary nature. The contrast of P on one hand and J and E on the other would soon become one of the central features and lasting inflection points for virtually all of pentateuchal scholarship.

With the work of de Wette and Hupfeld—and many others contemporaneous with them—the basic outline of a four-source theory for the Pentateuch emerged and took root in scholarship. Though Hupfeld, like many before him going back to Astruc, dealt primarily with Genesis, his arguments were soon extended to cover Exodus through Numbers as well. It was certainly clear to Hupfeld that P included not only the narrative up through the revelation of the divine name in Exod 6:2, but also the vast bulk of ritual and legal material that occupies the second half of Exodus (the construction of the tabernacle), all of Leviticus, and parts of Numbers. J and E also continued on past Genesis, though their identification was based largely on being what was left over once P, with its more readily identifiable content and diction, was removed. The separation of J and E, moreover, became increasingly

16. Hupfeld, *Quellen*, 98.

17. Hupfeld, *Quellen*, 193.

difficult once E, previously recognizable as the "Elohist" whose story did not conform to P's, introduced the divine name in Exod 3:14. Now the challenge became not to isolate E from P, but rather to isolate E from J among the mass of non-P material.

The basic situation was laid out by Theodor Nöldeke in 1869, who presented the state of the field after the first half of the nineteenth century. In brief, the Pentateuch could be divided into four main component parts. In chronological order:

1) P
2) J and E
3) the redactor responsible for combining P with J and E
4) D[18]

At the risk of some repetition, it is worth describing each of these parts individually, at least as they were understood at that time. Many of the conclusions reached two centuries ago have retained their force, even with various adjustments, down to the present.

To the modern reader, used to what has become the standard view of scholarship, it may be somewhat jarring to see P placed at the beginning of this scheme. Yet for much of the nineteenth century P was known either as the "Elohist" or, with increasing frequency, as "the basic writing" (German "Grundschrift") or "the original writing" ("Urschrift"). As we have seen, the chronological priority of P was based in part on Romantic ideas about literary development. If the presumed trend is from simple to more complex, then surely P, with its sparse storytelling and repetitive language, must have been earlier than J and E, with their complex narratives and more recognizable

18. Nöldeke, *Untersuchung*, 3–5.

literary artistry. P was understood to relate almost entirely facts (and figures—for many scholars the specificity of P's numbers, from the ages of characters to the census lists to the years, months, and even days of the wilderness wandering, were a sign of greater antiquity, and perhaps even authenticity). J and E, by contrast, were inclined toward both deeper characterization and emotional impact as well as more philosophical reflection. This is all readily apparent from the very first chapters of Genesis: P's creation story, in Gen 1, is described by Nöldeke as "the crowning glory" of P, in part because it exhibits standard P literary features: "the strictly systematic structure of the narrative . . . , the repetition of standard figures of speech, and the lack of clarity."[19] In the J creation account of Gen 2–3, on the other hand, we find "deep reflections on the basic questions of mankind."[20]

Beyond literary style, scholars understood P to be the earliest strand of the Pentateuch also because of what they viewed as the natural cultural and religious trajectory of ancient Israel. Bloody animal sacrifice, purity regulations, mysterious rites and rituals—these were all seen as bearing the mark of relative antiquity, as the ancient elemental features of a simple type of faith and worship. The priestly sacrificial system was so seemingly transactional, so patently material, that it must have been, in relative terms, primitive. As Nöldeke put it: "It would also be a strange phenomenon if early antiquity marked a higher stage of religious development among the Israelites than later times. In the end, the consequence would be that the great prophets, the bearers of tremendous

19. Nöldeke, *Untersuchung*, 7 (translation mine).

20. Nöldeke, *Untersuchung*, 133.

spiritual progress, would have coarsened religion."[21] This contrast, between the priestly and the prophetic, would, as we will see, come to be fundamental in the discussion of the Pentateuch's compositional history.

If P was the earliest and simplest source by virtue of being mostly facts and figures and ritual instructions, lacking in life and warmth, then J was identifiably later for all the opposite reasons. Here were characterization, ethical reflection, stories with morals. Here was continuity and thematic development over long stretches of text. As Hupfeld described it, "The presentation is generally characterized by greater richness, artistry and development: richer furnishing with motifs, character traits, illustrative circumstances and other details, tension of interest through complications, difficulties, tying up knots and their solution."[22] Here was, in short, the higher literary style that P was so clearly lacking. In J one could also find an advanced sensibility: "a significantly more pronounced theocractic consciousness, a stronger feeling of the advantage of the Israelite people and a more determined striving to emphasize it, . . . a messianic relationship to the salvation of 'all the peoples of the earth' in the blessing of the patriarchs . . . an advanced reflection on the phenomena of the human world and nature . . . a more developed theology and anthropology or psychological experience," as Hupfeld put it.[23] Note that Hupfeld too brings in the prophets as a point of comparison, in this case, for J, in a positive sense: J "already on the whole shares the point of view of the prophets and prophetic historiography."[24]

21. Nöldeke, *Untersuchung*, 133.

22. Hupfeld, *Quellen*, 97.

23. Hupfeld, *Quellen*, 95–96.

24. Hupfeld, *Quellen*, 95.

The baseline assumption is that the prophets represent the high-water mark of Israelite religion, and that the closer to the prophets a source seems to be, the later it is. It seems more than likely that this view, in turn, is dependent on Protestant Christianity's admiration for the prophetic literature, with its direct access to the deity and its ostensible rejection of the sacrificial rituals of the priestly writings (see, e.g., Isa 1:11: "What need have I for all your sacrifices?, says Yahweh").

E, for its part, occupied an uneasy middle ground. It was distinguishable from P on narrative grounds, despite using the same divine name, as Hupfeld showed. It was separable from J because of its use of "Elohim" rather than "Yahweh," but was stylistically and theologically very similar. E was like a rib removed from the side of P and almost immediately reinserted into the side of J. Even Hupfeld, who isolated it in the first place, and demonstrated that it must have been an independent document, drew contrasts between P and "the later sources," lumping J and E together. As a result, despite Hupfeld's arguments, subsequent scholars would have no difficulty imagining E as perhaps independent, yes, but still for all practical purposes as a part of J:

> I do not regard these two consistently organically connected source writings as independent of one another, but in my opinion the most brilliant of all pentateuchic writers, the Jehovist, uses as a main source that Elohist, an excellent narrator who undoubtedly belongs to the kingdom of Ephraim, and took from it but in an independent way, so that what belongs to the Jehovist himself and what he

> borrowed from the Elohist cannot always be clearly distinguished.[25]

Though Hupfeld had concentrated on contradictions in the narrative to separate E from P, the broad interest of scholarship—including Hupfeld—was to use literary style and theological perspective both to identify and, crucially, to date the pentateuchal sources. As long as these were the aims of interpreters, E was destined to exist in limbo, both recognizable and indistinguishable. This unfortunate position would come to define, and ultimately threaten, the status of E.

Finally, D was widely recognized as the latest of the pentateuchal sources, as de Wette had argued. Stylistically it was verbose and formal; theologically, with its demand for centralized worship, it moved beyond the earlier sources; and literarily it demonstrated knowledge of, dependence on, and correction of the narratives found in the preceding books.

Perhaps the defining feature of this era of source-critical inquiry was the close connection between the literary identification of the sources and the desire to place them in chronological order. A number of rationales might be suggested for this situation. Though the scholarly procedure was basically literary, the underlying problem was still seen as a historical one. Scholars in this period were still waging an intellectual battle against the traditional confessional views of the Pentateuch. Mosaic authorship was at its heart a historical claim; for the literary arguments to be successful, they too had to fight on the historical battlefield. Or, to put it another way: the value of literary analysis was to be found in its historical

25. Nöldeke, *Untersuchung*, 3.

payoff. It was still understood that the object of biblical scholarship was to uncover the truth about the past. Thus, as we have seen, for many scholars the literary history was closely aligned with the Bible's own representation of Israel's political, cultural, and religious history.

As we have also seen repeatedly, at the root of almost all scholarly reconstruction of the Pentateuch's composition was a Romantic notion of the text as a direct reflection of Israelite culture. In this sense the literary and the historical could hardly be separated: to describe one was to describe the other. Because Romanticism understood culture to develop in a recognizable and even predictable manner, from simple to complex, from natural to political, the pentateuchal sources also had to be set in a developmental scheme. Tied to this was a specifically Protestant value system. As noted above, the prophets were given pride of place as the greatest theological achievement of ancient Israel, and thus were placed later in the schema, closest to the advent of Jesus (it is no coincidence that this is also reflected in the order of the Christian biblical canon, in which the prophets are placed at the end of the Old Testament). Less obviously but just as commonly, the earliest pentateuchal strand, the priestly writings, were identified with Judaism.

> For later Judaism, the parts of the Pentateuch that came from the *Grundschrift* became the true basis. The other parts would not have offered sufficient material for the presentation of the peculiar hierarchically legal structure; only through that did Judaism acquire the specific character which made its extension to other peoples absolutely impractical.[26]

26. Nöldeke, *Untersuchung*, 142.

The literary analysis was part of a broader cultural claim, one that held up prophecy and Protestantism and implicitly denigrated priesthood and Judaism. The Romantic framework of chronological development, and the historical claims it entailed, was indispensable for drawing this broader contrast. While the terms would radically change in the next stage of scholarship, this fundamental discussion would continue to sit at the center of the debate.

CASE STUDY. GENESIS 28:10–22 (HUPFELD)

Hupfeld's treatment of our case study passage is considerably more complicated than that of Astruc. He identifies two sources, rather than one, though neither is perfectly complete. His analysis is as follows, in which plain text indicates J, and italics indicates his "younger Elohist," what would come to be called E.

> [10]Jacob left Beersheba and went toward Haran.
> [11]*He came to a certain place and stayed there for*
> *the night, because the sun had set. Taking one of*
> *the stones of the place, he put it under his head*
> *and lay down in that place.* [12]*And he dreamed*
> *that there was a stairway set up on the earth, the*
> *top of it reaching to heaven, and the angels of God*
> *were ascending and descending on it.* [13]And Yah-
> weh stood beside him and said, "I am Yahweh,
> the God of Abraham your father and the God
> of Isaac; the land on which you lie I will give to
> you and to your offspring, [14]and your offspring
> shall be like the dust of the earth, and you shall
> spread abroad to the west and to the east and to
> the north and to the south, and all the families
> of the earth shall be blessed in you and in your
> offspring. [15]Know that I am with you and will
> keep you wherever you go and will bring you

> back to this land, for I will not leave you until
> I have done what I have promised you.” 16Then
> Jacob woke from his sleep and said, “Surely
> Yahweh is in this place—and I did not know it!”
> 17*And he was afraid and said, “How awesome is*
> *this place! This is none other than the house of*
> *God, and this is the gate of heaven.”* 18*So Jacob*
> *rose early in the morning, and he took the stone*
> *that he had put under his head and set it up for a*
> *pillar and poured oil on the top of it.* 19He called
> that place Bethel, but the name of the city was
> Luz at the first. 20*Then Jacob made a vow, say-*
> *ing, “If God will be with me and will keep me in*
> *this way that I go and will give me bread to eat*
> *and clothing to wear,* 21*so that I come again to*
> *my father’s house in peace, then Yahweh shall be*
> *my god,* 22*and this stone, which I have set up for*
> *a pillar, shall be God’s house, and of all that you*
> *give me I will surely give one-tenth to you.”*

Hupfeld is far more attentive than Astruc both to the internal logic of the story and to the connections between it and other passages in Genesis. He begins with the link between this episode and the beginning of Gen 35, Jacob’s return to Bethel. Genesis 35:1–7, Hupfeld had already decided, is from the “younger Elohist,” as it consistently uses the title “Elohim,” but cannot be from the “older Elohist,” that is, P, which has its own contradictory story of Jacob naming Bethel in 35:9–15. Thus at least the parts of our passage that are directly connected to Gen 35 must also be from E. Key for Hupfeld is the vow at the end of the passage. Jacob asks for a safe journey, and promises upon his return to dedicate this spot as a cultic site, which is precisely what Hupfeld sees fulfilled in Gen 35:1–7. Thus 28:20–22 must also be from E. As the vow in 28:22 mentions the stone that Jacob used as a pillow, so all of the references to that stone must be E as well: 28:11 and 28:18. The dream in 28:12 belongs to E—Jacob is sleeping on his stone pillow, after all, and Hupfeld also notes that dreams are a frequent mode of divine communication in E. And, finally, Jacob's exclamation in 28:17 is also E, containing as it does the first use of the phrase "house of God," which returns in the vow in 28:22. So much for Hupfeld's E.

J, in Hupfeld's view, began with 28:10, because the destination of Haran, where Rebekah's family lives, is taken directly from the J story in Gen 27. The divine speech in 28:13–15 is also from J: as with Astruc, the prominent use of the divine name, Yahweh, is unavoidable. Moreover, Hupfeld points out that the content of the speech, the promise to Jacob, looks like other J promise passages (such as Gen 13:14–16). The use of "Yahweh" in 28:16 indicates that it too belongs to J. And finally, 28:19, the naming of Bethel, Hupfeld gives to J as well, seemingly because he reads it as the narrative payoff of Jacob's astonishment in 28:16.

The result of Hupfeld's analysis is two parallel narratives, each describing a theophany at Bethel, though told in two distinctive ways. Hupfeld himself recognized some of the weaknesses of his analysis. Notably, all of the mentions of Jacob going to sleep in 28:11–12—the night setting, the stone pillow, the dream—are in the E story, yet J too has Jacob waking from sleep (28:16), though there is otherwise no reference to Jacob sleeping previously in J. Hupfeld thus assumed that there was something missing from J, or that perhaps the two stories were thoroughly muddled at the beginning of 28:11. Seemingly unnoted by Hupfeld is the striking similarity between Yahweh's promise to Jacob in 28:15, "I am with you and will keep you wherever you go," from J, and Jacob's speech in 28:20,

"If God will be with me and will keep me in this way that I go," which he gives to E. Finally, Hupfeld, in reading the E story in Gen 28 along with what he saw as its continuation in Gen 35:1–7, created a situation in which Jacob is fleeing from Esau in E—but the narrative of Jacob stealing Esau's blessing, and Esau threatening to kill him, in Gen 27 belongs entirely to J. Thus, Hupfeld casually assumes that E must have had a similar story, though one that is nowhere preserved in our text.

We can see in Hupfeld's treatment of our case study passage a sharp eye for detail and for stylistic and thematic distinctions among the sources—understandable, since Hupfeld had an E to work with (unlike Astruc). At the same time, there remains a clear reliance on the evidence of the divine names in the separation of the sources, even more so than with Astruc. We can also see that, for Hupfeld, J and E are thought to be remarkably similar: not only so similar as to be at times indistinguishable (as at the beginning of 28:11), but assumed, even in the absence of the actual text, to have told the same stories (such as the conflict between Jacob and Esau and Jacob's subsequent flight).

GUIDING QUESTIONS

1. On what grounds did sources come to be distinguished from each other?
2. What criteria were used in this period for the relative dating of the various pentateuchal sources?
3. How would one describe the influence of Romantic thought on source criticism?

3

THE CLASSICAL PERIOD OF SOURCE CRITICISM

THOUGH THE SEPARATION AND identification of the sources of the Pentateuch was largely agreed on by the middle of the second half of the nineteenth century, the widespread acceptance of the documentary hypothesis came only at the end of the century, and has been associated ever since with one name: Julius Wellhausen. Wellhausen's accomplishment was not a new analysis of the text, nor a novel argument for its historical relevance, but rather the presentation of the entire concept in a straightforward and accessible framework. To this day, when most people are introduced to the documentary hypothesis, it is through the lens of Wellhausen's work. When the sources are described as "JEDP," that is Wellhausen. When J and E are lumped together, that is Wellhausen. When the sources are used to outline the chronological development of Israelite religion, that is Wellhausen. And when the rituals of Leviticus are decried as unnatural or legalistic, that too is Wellhausen. Though few if any of these ideas were his originally, it was Wellhausen who brought them to public attention, and whose writings have remained a landmark, obscuring those who preceded him.

It is our task in this chapter, then, to understand what exactly Wellhausen argued, and why. What ideas and intellectual trends did he build on, and why was his presentation of them so effective and compelling? How can we thoughtfully and critically engage with Wellhausen and his legacy?

We have already encountered many of the fundamentals of Wellhausen's argument. As noted above, the technical task of separating the sources and identifying them as J, E, P, and D—even if not by those exact names or sigla—was already well established by de Wette and Hupfeld, among others. Even in the initial identification of E by Hupfeld, as we have seen, the relationship of J and E had become complicated. Scholars had already begun organizing the sources chronologically on the basis of the perceived stage of Israelite religion that they might represent. Where Wellhausen really made a distinctive advance over previous scholarship was in his relocation of the priestly material from the earliest stage—the *Grundschrift*—to the latest. Even in this, however, Wellhausen was not the first to make the case.

For that, credit belongs to a contemporary: Karl Heinrich Graf. For Graf, the fundamental temporal division in the Pentateuch was between the narrative materials, broadly construed, and the ritual-legal texts of the priestly source. The former Graf understood to be pre-exilic, the latter post-exilic. In his first major statement on the topic, Graf simply removed the priestly legal material to the end of the line, thus suggesting a sequence of narrative complexes (J, E, and the narratives of P), Deuteronomy (D), and late ritual-legal texts (the P material from mid-Exodus through mid-Numbers).[1] Though this theory would nearly immediately be retracted, it nevertheless inaugurated a major new stage of source-critical discussion. In part because so much attention had been historically paid to Genesis, it had long been the narrative discrepancies among the sources that drove the compositional analysis, as seen most clearly in the work of Hupfeld. Graf, however, shifted scholarly attention to the legal portions of the Pentateuch. Here, he claimed—as Wellhausen would go on to more fully articulate—the development of Israelite religion could be plainly seen.

Almost as soon as Graf published his argument, it was challenged by some of his peers, who pointed out that the priestly writings could hardly be severed this way. As Nöldeke had argued, the overarching ideology of P was consistent across both narrative and law. It was a mere three years later that Graf made what would be among the most momentous analytical moves in the history of pentateuchal scholarship, relocating not only the laws but also the narratives of P from earliest to latest.[2] Graf thus gave us the order J/E-D-P, which has remained the standard, for better or worse, ever since. We may note that the earliest sources, J and E, are essentially interchangeable in this scheme. This is because it was no longer, as it had been for Hupfeld, the literary style of the sources that determined their order, but rather the laws and their representation of Israelite religion. Thus, the lateness of P's laws brought

1. Graf, *Geschichtlichen Bücher.*

2. Graf, "Grundschrift."

P's narrative along for the ride, while the earliness of the Covenant Code in Exod 21–23 made the attached narratives also early. It was of little difference, or even interest, to which of the earliest sources the Covenant Code belonged. The sequence that really mattered was, in the end, Covenant Code–Deuteronomy–priestly laws. The division of the Pentateuch into sources, and their relative dating, was now based primarily on the legal material, to which the narratives were then assigned.

It was not only the P source that thus underwent a significant reimagining in the work of Graf. J and E, having been so carefully separated by Hupfeld less than thirty years earlier, were now combined into a single phase, their narrative contradictions obscured by their common relative position vis-à-vis the laws of D and P. Though scholars would continue to recognize J and E as individual sources, it would become standard fare for the two to be treated together—and, indeed, for the ability to distinguish them, as we will see, to be increasingly doubted if not outright rejected.

It was this basic proposition—an early J and E, a middle-era D, and a late P—that Wellhausen would take up and popularize. In practical terms, this was done entirely through the lens of the law. Wellhausen looked at a few topics that recur across the three major legal collections—the place of worship, sacrifice, festivals, the priesthood and its perquisites—and he carefully argued that a clear and consistent development could be identified, moving from the Covenant Code (JE) to Deuteronomy to P.[3] To take a single example: Wellhausen observed that while the Covenant Code permits sacrifice to take place

3. Wellhausen, *Prolegomena*.

anywhere an Israelite may build an altar ("in every place where I cause my name to be remembered I will come to you and bless you," Exod 20:24), D centralizes worship in a single location: "Take care that you do not offer your burnt offerings at any place you happen to see. But only at the place that Yahweh will choose in one of your tribes—there you shall offer your burnt offerings" (Deut 12:13–14). P, for its part, is marked as later still by not even arguing for, but merely assuming, the centralization of worship, in its depiction of the single tabernacle in the wilderness (Exod 25–31; 35–40).

Wellhausen thus offered the fullest working out of de Wette's claim, cited in the previous chapter: "The various laws of the Pentateuch reflect different periods of time." This approach may have found a more favorable public reception in part because it seemed more solidly grounded than previous rationales for the relative dating of the sources. Literary style, which served as the guide for Hupfeld, could well be chalked up to aesthetic preferences, for both the biblical authors and the biblical reader. Here, however, was evidence that was seemingly based in actual ancient Israelite practices and theological positions. Similarly, though narrative inconsistencies, especially in Genesis, might be debatable, contradictions in practical matters, such as where Israelites were allowed to offer sacrifices, were considerably starker.

And yet: despite a presentation that lays claims to objective analysis of the textual data, Wellhausen's argument did not start from a neutral perspective on the text. It emerged from and participated in intellectual positions, explicit and implicit, that shaped and colored his conclusions. To understand Wellhausen, and indeed the entire documentary hypothesis that bore his name for the century that followed, we must understand the frameworks with which he was working, and the assumptions that he brought to the table.

Central—indeed, fundamental—to Wellhausen's analysis is an assumption that goes back to de Wette, and that has been shared by many scholars ever since: that the pentateuchal sources, though not historically accurate in their description of the period that they narrate, are in fact reasonably accurate snapshots of Israelite practices at the times of their composition. That is, P's ritual legislation, for example, while not at all realistic for the time of Moses (if there ever was such a time), can and should be taken as representative of sacrificial practices in the time of P. But Wellhausen, like those before him and for some time after, wrote with relatively little access to archaeological data that might shed light on the realities behind the text. We, however, can demonstrate that many, if not most, of the biblical laws seem to have little correlation with verifiable widespread Israelite practice. For all of P's insistence on ritual purity, for example, there is no archaeological evidence for any purity-related practices—such as ritual baths—prior to the second century BCE.[4] We thus have reason to doubt the very basis of Wellhausen's reconstruction.

We may, however, speculate on why Wellhausen, and so many others, did assume that the sources gave us access to actual Israelite practices. It seems quite likely that this assumption came about in a manner familiar to us from some of the earliest source critics. We may recall that for Astruc, Vater, and Ewald, while true Mosaic authorship was no longer sustainable there was still an implicit desire

4. Adler, *Origins*, 86.

to maintain the "authenticity," variously defined, of the Pentateuch. So too for Wellhausen, and for so many who fall under the umbrella term "historical critics." Confessional claims for the historicity of the Bible could be both rejected on their face and also, paradoxically, preserved. Though the story the Bible tells may not be true, the text still preserves a "truth," accessible through historical-critical analysis. Indeed, in a period before widespread archaeological efforts in Syro-Palestine, to decouple the text from the actual history would be to abandon any firm historical claims about ancient Israel altogether.

Wellhausen made no secret of the fact that his efforts were aimed at historical reconstruction. The book in which he presented his argument was, after all, called *Prolegomena to the History of Israel.* We should, however, credit Wellhausen with at least being clear about the separation of the two major elements of his work. Though most students are familiar with the *Prolegomena* (in part because it has been translated into English), Wellhausen did not begin with the historical reconstruction, but rather with the more traditional separation and identification of the sources, in an earlier (as yet untranslated) book, *The Composition of the Hexateuch.*[5] That is, Wellhausen did the purely literary analysis first, working through the entire Pentateuch, narrative and law alike. Only thereafter did he make historical claims on the basis of his source division. Many scholars, familiar only with the historical arguments, have confused and conflated the two steps. All too often (as we will see in later chapters) scholars begin with historical arguments and then do literary analysis on that basis, or, in challenging the dating of a given passage

5. Wellhausen, *Composition.*

or source they claim to have undermined the very existence of that source altogether.

Corollary to the assumption of historical realities lying behind the sources, and just as common, is the assumption that the sources were authoritative texts in ancient Israel. This is an assumption that goes back to well before Wellhausen—all the way to Astruc, in fact—but one that is rarely if ever defended by those who hold it. The sources were not merely records of particular historical periods, but were effectively national documents: J for the southern kingdom of Judah; E for the northern kingdom of Israel; D for the unified kingdom after the fall of the north in 722 BCE; P for the post-exilic hierocracy of the Second Temple period. As such they were also understood to have been written with knowledge of each other. J was first, but E knew and responded to J, D to the combined J/E, and P to all the others. (We may see in this an echo of de Wette's claim that D was composed on the basis of the "Mosaic History" in Genesis–Numbers. In Wellhausen's scheme, P simply took the place of D.) We may see here the same sort of desire to maintain the authority of the text in the face of advancing scholarly challenges to traditional claims. While the Pentateuch as a whole could no longer be viewed as the foundational document of ancient Israel, at least its constituent elements, one after another and in sequential combination, could be. There was, in other words, always some text that operated in a manner similar to that previously assigned to the Pentateuch, as a culturally prescriptive text. (Thus, again, the focus on the laws over the narratives.)

Tied to the understanding of the sources as authoritative and historically accurate snapshots of ancient

Israelite custom is, unsurprisingly, the Romantic notion of the sources as representing the development of Israelite culture, from naïve and "natural" to more mature and advanced. The major difference between Wellhausen and his predecessors, who, as we have seen repeatedly, also partake in this Romantic view of the Bible, is the shift from literature to religion. Wellhausen was a student of Ewald, who was, as noted above, among the first to view the text through an evolutionary lens. He also wrote in the immediate wake of Darwin's theories of natural evolution, which were enormously influential across the sciences and the humanities alike. Unlike Hupfeld and others, Wellhausen did not focus on a perceived development in literary form or style to determine the sequence of the sources, but rather on the imagined development in Israelite religious practice and thought. "In the Pentateuch the elements follow upon one another and from one another precisely as the steps of the development demonstrably do in history."[6] While preserving the basic idea of a discernible evolution from simple to complex, this shift resulted in a reorientation and reordering of the sources. While P may employ a relatively "simple" literary style—as Hupfeld and Nöldeke both noted—its description of the cult is undeniably more complex than that of the other sources.

Romantic notions of cultural development, however, are accompanied by value judgments that are not always pegged directly to chronological progress. We may recall de Wette's unflattering description of D's style as both "refined" and "corrupted" as compared with the "simple" and "natural" style of the earlier sources. By contrast, Hupfeld considered the later J style to be fuller

6. Wellhausen, *Prolegomena*, 13.

and livelier than that of the earlier P. Looking somewhat beyond style, Nöldeke placed P early in part because it was so different in religious outlook from the prophets, which he viewed as the high-water mark of Israelite religious thought, and thus must have been late. These varied perspectives reveal one of the underlying tensions in Romanticism: the competing allure of early and "natural" cultural expression, on one hand, and the idea of inexorable cultural progress on the other. How does one scheme encompass both of these values?

On a surface level, Wellhausen seems to lean strongly toward the former. While he argues that Israelite religion progressed from simple to complex, from J/E to P, he makes no secret of his preference for the earlier over the later. Most important for Wellhausen (indeed, perhaps overriding his actual textual analysis) is the relative positions of "the law"—by which he means the priestly legislation—and "the prophets." If for Nöldeke the prophets had to come last because they were the highest form of Israelite religion, for Wellhausen they had to come first—and for the same reason. J and E Wellhausen understood as contemporary with the prophets: dating "from the golden age of Hebrew literature, to which the finest parts of Judges, Samuel, and Kings, and the oldest extant prophetical writings also belong."[7] (Note the value judgment in the phrase "the finest parts.")

The priority of the prophets over the law was not a result of Wellhausen's analysis, but in fact a prerequisite to it. For this we need not speculate. Wellhausen opens the *Prolegomena* with a brief autobiographical note in which he says so openly. He tells the reader that though he began with a fair acquaintance with the prophetic literature, his

7. Wellhausen, *Prolegomena*, 9.

enjoyment of it "was marred by the Law; it did not bring them any nearer me, but intruded itself uneasily."[8] Having an *a priori* distaste for the law, Wellhausen admits that, upon hearing Graf's suggestion that the law was in fact late, "almost without knowing his reasons for the hypothesis, I was prepared to accept it; I readily acknowledged to myself the possibility of understanding Hebrew antiquity without the book of the Torah."[9]

It takes no great insight to recognize that Wellhausen's preference for the prophets over the law, broadly speaking, is not idiosyncratic to him but mirrors the traditional Christian, and especially Protestant, view of the Old Testament. The very order of the Christian Old Testament evinces this preference, with the law set at the beginning, in the conceptually distant past, and the prophets placed at the end, where they are read as anticipating Jesus and the New Testament. For nearly two millennia Christianity had rejected the law of Moses—with the notable exception of the Ten Commandments, which are, perhaps conveniently for Wellhausen, one of the few legal texts to be found in his earlier sources, J/E. Wellhausen's "enjoyment" of the prophets, as compared to the law, is largely indistinguishable from basic Christian belief.

It is through this lens that we can see how Wellhausen upholds the other Romantic value, that of cultural progress. While the prophets may be early in Israel's religious history, they are in fact also the endpoint of it, as they are revived in the person of Jesus—they are made part of the Christian story. What, then, of the law? It was effectively removed from the history of Christianity and assigned, rather, to a stage of Israel's cultural movement

8. Wellhausen, *Prolegomena*, 3.

9. Wellhausen, *Prolegomena*, 3–4.

away from authentic religious expression and toward the legalism of Judaism.

We can see in Wellhausen not a simple linear progression, but in fact two parallel cycles. First is that of ancient Israel: a "golden age" of the prophets and early pentateuchal materials that gradually devolved into increasing ritualistic legalism, a religion of rules and of priests who imposed them and set themselves as intermediaries between the people and God. Judaism continued this downward trend, but a new cycle began with the advent of Christianity, which returned to the prophetic origins of Israelite religion, as it were. The second cycle, which Wellhausen does not articulate directly but which patently underlies his work, is then that of Christianity itself: a "golden age" of Jesus and his followers, akin to the prophetic era of Israel. And just as ancient Israel had done, Christianity gradually devolved into increasing ritualistic legalism, a religion of rules and of priests who imposed them and set themselves as intermediaries between the people and God—that is, Catholicism. In this scheme, Protestantism—which is to say, Wellhausen—represents the cyclical return to the more direct and natural religion of early Christianity and also of early Israel. The source-critical analysis that "rediscovers" the originality, antiquity, and authenticity of the prophets (and J/E, with the Ten Commandments) over against the degraded religious expression of the law and its priests is in no sense mere objective historical scholarship. It is, rather, a deeply value-laden expression of Protestant Christianity. It is source criticism in service of the church.

Here we are faced with the task of understanding not merely where Wellhausen's ideas came from, but also some of the unfortunate facets of his argument. For while Wellhausen may have had his sights set on promoting Protestantism over the Catholic church, his writing takes aim entirely at Judaism. Wellhausen denigrates "the law" and Judaism equally and often simultaneously. "The sacred action came to be regarded as essentially perfect by virtue of its own efficacy in being performed by the priest. . . . The connection of all this with the Judaising tendency to remove God to a distance from man, it may be added, is clear."[10] The later priestly texts, and Judaism after it, are viewed not only as subsequent to but directly antagonistic toward the "truth":

> The theocratic ideal was from the exile onwards the centre of all thought and effort, and it annihilated the sense for objective truth, all regard and interest for the actual facts as they had been handed down. It is well known that there have never been more audacious history-makers than the Rabbins [Wellhausen's strange term for the rabbis]. But . . . this evil propensity goes back to a very early time, its root the dominating influence of the Law, being the root of Judaism itself.[11]

As noted above, one of Wellhausen's aims seems to be the very severing of P, and Judaism, from some pure notion of ancient Israel:

> Judaism, which realised the Mosaic constitution and carried it out logically, left no free scope for the individual; but in ancient Israel the divine right did not attach to the institution, but was in the Creator Spirit, in individuals. Not only

10. Wellhausen, *Prolegomena*, 79.
11. Wellhausen, *Prolegomena*, 160–61.

> did they speak like the prophets, they also acted like the judges and kings, from their own free impulse, not in accordance with an outward norm, and yet, or just because of this, in the Spirit of Jehovah.[12]

P, the law, and Judaism, in this view, have abandoned the "spirit" of ancient Israel. Literature, in the Romantic sense, is meant to preserve and convey the "spirit" of the people. What Wellhausen has done here, then, is effectively to state that P, and its successor Judaism, is not in fact a representative text of ancient Israelite culture, but is an imposition forced upon Israel by the institution of the priesthood. For a Protestant reader, this is all familiar territory. So too for Jews.

The antisemitism of Wellhausen's writing cannot be separated from his project as a whole. It is present both in the autobiographical prologue that sets out his theological preferences and in his detailed analysis of ancient Israelite religion. Nor is it merely tangential: the prioritization, chronologically and conceptually, of the prophets over the law is the very *raison d'être* of the *Prolegomena*. Less than fifty years before the Holocaust, one of the most influential works in the history of biblical scholarship was built on and directly promoted the view that Judaism was an illegitimate and inauthentic religion, and that the book it claimed as the core of its faith in fact belonged more truly to Christianity.

In this light, it is worth reflecting on the instant and abiding popularity of Wellhausen's presentation. As we have seen, Wellhausen built on much that came before him. When one surveys the history of source criticism,

12. Wellhausen, *Prolegomena*, 412.

as we have, his argument is singularly uncomplicated: P belongs at the end, rather than the beginning. That's basically it. And yet Wellhausen caught on in a way that no one else had, and his continues to be the standard understanding of the history of the Pentateuch's composition. In generous terms, this is perhaps because—and this is certainly the case—Wellhausen was able to take for granted, at least in the *Prolegomena*, the results of all the preceding technical literary analyses and concentrate only on offering a clear and coherent narrative reconstruction of Israelite religion. A more cynical reader, however, might wonder whether what was so appealing about Wellhausen was precisely that which now seems most offensive: that it spoke to a Protestant audience's desire to see themselves as upholding the authentic principles of ancient Israel in stark contrast to the decadence of Judaism and Catholicism.

It is perhaps telling that some of the firmest resistance to Wellhausen came from Jewish scholars, notably Yehezkel Kaufmann in the mid-twentieth century.[13] Yet even in his rebuttal of Wellhausen's blatant anti-Jewish stance, Kaufmann challenged neither the underlying division of the pentateuchal sources nor, in fact, the basic conceptual underpinnings of Wellhausen's scheme. Kaufmann argued, against Wellhausen, for the chronological priority of P, but for essentially the same reasons that Wellhausen claimed priority for the prophets: because P is most similar to Judaism, and should thus hold pride of place as the earliest and most authentic form of Israelite religion. The desire to find a narrative underlying the biblical text—not the story *in* the text, but the story *of* the text—and a narrative, moreover,

13. Kaufmann, *Religion of Israel.*

that leads teleologically to the scholar in question, or to the scholar's community, is a powerful one.

This is what Wellhausen offered: a way of reading the Pentateuch that undermined traditional claims of authorship and authority but replaced them with new claims of authorship and authority. The Pentateuch remained a source for historical truth, of a type that conformed more closely to the Romantic post-Enlightenment perspective of nineteenth-century Protestant Europe.

It is a small irony, perhaps, that any overview of source criticism has to spend so much time and energy coming to terms with Wellhausen and the *Prolegomena*. He is, of course, unavoidable: he remains the linchpin of pentateuchal scholarship. But what he is famous for, and what we have devoted much of this chapter to understanding, is not in fact source criticism at all. As noted above, Wellhausen was careful to separate his task into two discrete steps: first, the source criticism, the detailed technical analysis of the text and its sources; and, second, the reconstruction of the history of Israelite religion that is based on that source division. Wellhausen didn't conflate the two, but most subsequent readers have. Few people, even scholars, have read Wellhausen's source analysis. Almost everyone in the field, and many outside it, are familiar with his periodization of Israelite religion. This is a shame, not only because Wellhausen was a fine reader of the text whose analysis deserves attention, but because it has led to source criticism being understood largely as a set of claims about cultural chronology, about dating and development, rather than as an attempt to make sense of the unique literary features of the Pentateuch.

As we will see in the chapters that follow, Wellhausen's model has remained fundamental in virtually all subsequent scholarship—but it has not gone unchallenged, in ways both minor and major.

CASE STUDY. GENESIS 28:10–22 (WELLHAUSEN)

Like Hupfeld, Wellhausen finds evidence in our passage of both J and E; like Hupfeld, he asserts that the editing of the two together has resulted in an imperfect separation. While there are minor differences in their analyses, the most prominent is the role that Wellhausen gives to the redactor of J and E. This is in line with his understanding of the Pentateuch as something of a rolling corpus, each stage and each redaction represented not just by the mechanical combination of sources but by their intentional and theologically minded integration. In Wellhausen's analysis presented below, J is in plain text, E is in italics, and what is assigned to the redactor of J and E is underlined.

> 10*Jacob left Beersheba and went toward Haran.*
> 11*He came to a certain place and stayed there for*
> *the night, because the sun had set. Taking one of*
> *the stones of the place, he put it under his head*
> *and lay down in that place.* 12*And he dreamed*
> *that there was a stairway set up on the earth, the*
> *top of it reaching to heaven, and the angels of God*
> *were ascending and descending on it.* 13And Yah-
> weh stood beside him and said, "I am Yahweh,
> the God of Abraham your father and the God
> of Isaac; the land on which you lie I will give to
> you and to your offspring, 14and your offspring
> shall be like the dust of the earth, and you shall
> spread abroad to the west and to the east and to
> the north and to the south, and all the families

> of the earth shall be blessed in you and in your
> offspring. [15]Know that I am with you and will
> keep you wherever you go and will bring you
> back to this land, for I will not leave you until
> I have done what I have promised you." [16]Then
> Jacob woke from his sleep and said, "Surely
> Yahweh is in this place—and I did not know it!"
> [17]*And he was afraid and said, "How awesome is*
> *this place! This is none other than the house of*
> *God, and this is the gate of heaven."* [18]*So Jacob*
> *rose early in the morning, and he took the stone*
> *that he had put under his head and set it up for a*
> *pillar and poured oil on the top of it.* [19]He called
> that place Bethel, but the name of the city was
> Luz at the first. [20]*Then Jacob made a vow, say-*
> *ing, "If God will be with me and will keep me in*
> *this way that I go and will give me bread to eat*
> *and clothing to wear,* [21]*so that I come again to*
> *my father's house in peace,* then Yahweh shall be
> my god, [22]*and this stone, which I have set up for*
> *a pillar, shall be God's house, and of all that you*
> *give me I will surely give one-tenth to you."*

Wellhausen takes the majority of the passage as being from E, with only 28:13–16 and the first clause of 28:19 being from J. Building explicitly on Hupfeld's analysis, Wellhausen adds further narrative reasons for the division of the text. He points out that if Yahweh speaks directly to Jacob in 28:13–15, there is no need for the angels. When 28:13–16 are removed, the continuity is clear: Jacob sees the angels ascending and descending, and realizes that this place is a nexus between heaven and earth. The naming of Bethel in 28:19 Wellhausen reads as a doublet of 28:22, where Jacob calls the place a "house of God."

Yet in addition to these observations, Wellhausen offers another familiar rationale: the divine names. The story uses "Elohim" everywhere but 28:13–16, which exclusively use "Yahweh." The exception to the rule is the final clause of 28:21, "then Yahweh shall be my god," an ostensible problem that he solves by attributing it to the redactor. The second half of 28:19 he also gives to the redactor, seeing it as a later gloss on the place-name Bethel. The third redactional insertion is to be found in the final word of 28:14, "and in your offspring." This is perhaps the least obvious but most telling of the later additions: Wellhausen removes it from J because, in his view, J's understanding of the patriarchal promise is that the nations of the earth will bless themselves by Abraham's name, while the redactor's position is that the nations will be blessed via Abraham and his offspring. On this Wellhausen comments, "Whoever put J and E together here will definitely have given something of his own to it."[14] Here we can see how his concept of the theologically minded redactor impacts his analysis.

Like Hupfeld, Wellhausen recognizes that his J story is incomplete—even more so than in Hupfeld's treatment. But because Wellhausen has a much more active redactor than Hupfeld, this isn't a problem for him. He may be able to identify J and E elements here, but his general position is that the two are usually very difficult to distinguish: "in such a tight interweaving that a clean separation is completely unthinkable."[15] It is in part Wellhausen's inability to separate J and E that leads to his theory of an active redactor. At the same time, it allows him—or perhaps requires him—to presume, like Hupfeld but even more so, that J and E told essentially the same story, even when most of it is missing. "In 28:10–22 we have an almost complete piece

14. Wellhausen, *Composition*, 31.

15. Wellhausen, *Composition*, 30.

from E, and at the same time a large fragment from J, which proves that J contained the same story and in the same place."[16] What's more, Wellhausen assumes that "the great similarity between J and E" extends not only to the idea of a theophany at Bethel, but to the reason for Jacob being there in the first place: "It follows by inference that both J and E also reported the reason for Jacob's flight"—though note that there is nothing in Wellhausen's J that mentions Jacob fleeing anything or anyone—"without which they would be unmotivated and incomprehensible. In both stories there must necessarily be a story like Genesis 27."[17] And so Wellhausen goes on to divide Gen 27 into two sources as well, thus breaking with Hupfeld.

Though Wellhausen's name is usually synonymous with a simple four-source theory, we can see here how his analysis is considerably more complex than that of his predecessors. His J and E are so closely parallel as to often be indistinguishable, and significant parts of what were previously attributed to either one are now given to a redactor who intervenes to promote his own theological ideas.

GUIDING QUESTIONS

1. On what grounds did Wellhausen (and Graf before him) argue for P as the latest of the pentateuchal sources?
2. What is the relationship between the biblical text and the history of Israelite religion for Wellhausen?
3. How much of Wellhausen's argument is dependent on evolutionary and antisemitic thought?

16. Wellhausen, *Composition*, 32.
17. Wellhausen, *Composition*, 32.

4

COMPLICATIONS

Addition and Subtraction

THE FIRST HALF OF the twentieth century saw a flourishing of new approaches to source criticism. Though Wellhausen's influence was undeniable, the field was deeply affected by the rise of a new consideration in the study of the Pentateuch, and the Hebrew Bible as a whole: the role of orality and pre-literary traditions. Already Vater, as we have seen, had anticipated this topic, suggesting that a world of Israelite oral tradition lay behind much of the material in the Pentateuch. Wellhausen, too, had kept open the possibility that there was substantial pre-literary development at work prior to the creation of the pentateuchal sources. But it was at the turn of the century that these ideas were subject to formal study, and with that study came a variety of complications to the documentary hypothesis.

The most significant figure in reshaping the landscape of source criticism in light of oral tradition was the German scholar Hermann Gunkel. Gunkel was heavily influenced by Scandinavian research into the development of folk tales, such as that of the Grimm brothers, and was a charter member of what was known as the "history of religions" school, which looked outside the Bible to identify the cultural origins of biblical stories and ideas. In 1901, Gunkel published the first edition of his massive commentary on Genesis.[1] It was here that he put forward a new understanding of the text's origins, focusing less on the content and more directly on the form, or genre, of each passage. Each form—myth, legend, etiology, etc.—could be traced back, according to Gunkel, to a setting in the life of the Israelite community in which such types of stories would have been orally created and transmitted.

The form of a given passage was necessarily an abstraction of it. It is not the origins of the text itself that are in question, but of the underlying genre in which it participated. Yet, in generating these abstracted forms, Gunkel also opened the door for a developmental approach to Israelite literature, furthering the Romantic notion of cultural evolution over time. Oral traditions were understood to be, unsurprisingly, older (they were preliterary, after all), and, importantly, simpler: "The earliest story-tellers were not capable of constructing artistic works of any considerable extent," Gunkel wrote.[2] There is more than a hint of Orientalism here. What this meant for Gunkel was that one could attempt to determine the relative age of biblical texts by their brevity: "the briefer a legend, the greater the probability that we have it in

1. Gunkel, *Genesis übersetzt*.

2. Gunkel, *Legends*, 47.

its original form."[3] By contrast, later writers were more expansive, both in their retellings of earlier traditions and in their desire to bring those traditions together into something closer to what we might call "history," a continuous narrative of Israel's past.

Gunkel accepted without hesitation the conclusions of Wellhausen and his predecessors with regard to the literary formation of Genesis: J, E, and P. These, however, he saw as not the beginning but the end of a history. Gunkel saw J and E, the chronologically earliest sources, as the first history writers, less true authors than collectors of preexisting oral traditions. (P, by contrast, was a real author, forming a thoroughgoing and coherent story even while building on early materials.) The real history of Genesis was to be found not in the sources but in what preceded them: the individual stories that J and E gathered together (the influence of the Grimms is readily apparent).

While Wellhausen used the pentateuchal sources to create a scheme of the development of Israelite religion, Gunkel used the oral traditions behind those sources to paint a picture of the development of Israelite culture. This entailed the shift from orality to writing, to be sure; but it also allowed for a more nuanced view of the differentiations among the various written instantiations of a given form. In creating an abstracted formal or generic template, Gunkel suggested that we could see more clearly how much a given literary text adhered to or deviated from that template. In this way we could identify how early or late, how naïve or advanced, a given version might be. An example of this is the three stories in Genesis of a patriarch passing off his wife as his sister in a foreign court. It was widely accepted that two of these, in Genesis

3. Gunkel, *Legends*, 47.

12 and 26, belonged to J, while the third, in Genesis 20, was from E. But for Gunkel, looking past the sources, there were formal differences even in the two J versions of the story. This, and similar examples, led him to postulate that the J source was in fact itself not a unity, but could be divided into editions or layers: J^a and J^b, as he termed them. Regardless of the defensibility of such a claim, it is the very fact of the claim itself that is of importance for the history of the field. A relatively simple four-source picture from Wellhausen is suddenly complicated. What's more, the potential for further complication still is apparent: if J could be split into multiple layers, then so could any other source; so too, perhaps, even J^a and J^b. And once J becomes two Js, one might naturally ask what it is that holds J together as a source at all.

The decades after Gunkel would see the study of the Pentateuch move in multiple different directions, as the field that had coalesced around Wellhausen splintered. In what follows in this chapter we will trace three of the main trends, beginning with Gunkel's immediate intellectual successors, the German scholars Gerhard Von Rad and Martin Noth. Von Rad and Noth continued to work with the pre-literary stages of the text's formation, but shifted their attention from the generic literary forms to the content of those forms: what came to be known as the traditions of the text.

Von Rad closely followed Gunkel in the assessment of J as a collector of material more than as an author proper.[4] While Gunkel worked with the individual episodes of J, Von Rad took a more holistic view. He suggested that prior to J there had been a common story of Israel's early

4. Von Rad, "Form-Critical Problem."

history, but one that, crucially, had not included the Sinai event. The combination of the patriarchal and exodus themes with the law-giving at Sinai was, in Von Rad's view, J's innovation. Though he used the language of form criticism, Von Rad changed the terms: he was concerned not with the types of literary genres employed by J but with the actual stories themselves. How did the overarching story of the Pentateuch—primeval history, patriarchs, Joseph, Egypt, exodus, Sinai, wilderness—come to be?

It was Noth who provided the fullest answer to this question, inaugurating what has come to be termed "tradition history."[5] The pentateuchal story, he argued, was an assemblage of once-independent traditional blocks. Thus, the patriarchal traditions had a prehistory separate from that of the exodus and conquest traditions, for example. Each major traditional block, in turn, had a prehistory of its own. Within the patriarchal traditions, those of Abraham, Isaac, and Jacob were all distinctive and originally unaffiliated with each other. Just as Gunkel had taken episodes from the text and reduced them to their abstracted literary form, Noth took episodes from the text and reduced them to their earliest possible independent content. From the overarching pentateuchal narrative one could isolate the theme of the patriarchs; within that, the collective traditions of Jacob; within that, the specific traditions of Jacob's conflict with Esau, Jacob's encounter with Laban, Jacob's founding of a cultic site at Bethel, and so on.

While Gunkel used his analysis to propose a history of the development of Israelite culture, Noth looked to reconstruct the history of Israel as a people. Each of these smallest traditions could be linked with a stage of Israel's

5. Noth, *Pentateuchal Traditions.*

history. The tradition of Jacob and Esau was a narrativized retrojection of Israel's relationship with Edom. The tradition of Jacob and Laban was similarly about Israel and Aram. The Bethel narrative is the etiology, or explanatory story, for the existence of the sanctuary at Bethel. Not only the independent traditions but also their combinations were data in the reconstruction of the past. The Jacob and Abraham traditions coming together to form the patriarchal complex was attributed to the real-world uniting, probably through intermarriage, of those early Israelites who traced their ancestry back to a figure named Jacob with those who traced their ancestry to Abraham.

As with Gunkel, on the surface Von Rad and Noth did not challenge the source-critical status quo—indeed, they too accepted the standard Wellhausen model, and their approaches have been understood, as the names "form criticism" and "tradition criticism" suggest, to be doing something different altogether. Yet their work, like Gunkel's, had significant implications for the source-critical project. The change of focus from the source to its constituent elements changed the way that the pentateuchal material was approached. Prior to Gunkel, Von Rad, and Noth, it was the canonical text that was taken as a given, and the sources that required definition. With their approaches, by contrast, it was the pentateuchal sources, according to Wellhausen's scheme, that were the given, and the components thereof that required definition. And just as the discovery of the literary sources naturally gave rise to the question of how they had been brought together to form the Pentateuch, so too the discovery of pre-literary materials led to the question of how they had been combined to form the literary sources. Put together, this resulted in a change of analytical direction: building up from the pieces, rather than pulling apart the whole.

Though it would take some time to become apparent, the attention given by these scholars to the oral stories behind the written sources fundamentally reshaped the nature of the source-critical enterprise. Though they worked with Wellhausen's source model, their work has distinct resonances with the fragmentary approach of Vater. It is, essentially, atomizing: taking the individual episode as the basic literary unit. Where these episodes came from, how they developed over time, and how they were combined into the sources as we have them—these were their questions. And while they took for granted that the individual episodes came together to form J, E, and P, their approach opened the door for a radical shift in perspective among scholars who did not share that assumption, as will see further.

We can also see in Gunkel, Von Rad, and Noth a continuing reflex of the loss of the Pentateuch's traditional authority. Wellhausen, following especially de Wette, had already made clear that what the pentateuchal sources offer us is not an accurate narrative history of ancient Israel but rather insight into the social and cultural circumstances of the period(s) when they were written. For Gunkel, the generic literary forms that underlie the sources allow us to go further back, into the history of Israelite culture before the sources were written. For Noth, the traditions that stand behind the pentateuchal stories give us access to the history of Israelite society and politics. Neither Gunkel nor Noth proposed that the early history of Israel was in fact that told in the Pentateuch—yet the Pentateuch remained for them the text from which that early history could be derived. The text was still, or, perhaps better, again, a reliable source of truth about the most distant past.

As scholarship progressed down the road of pre-literary analysis, it became, necessarily, more and more untethered from the pentateuchal text. The canonical text is apparent on the page; the sources, though still represented on the page, are scholarly reconstructions; the forms and traditions behind the sources are entirely conjectural. Yet it was in these conjectures that these scholars found meaning. The canonical text was a mere mash-up of extant texts, and a late literary product. The sources gave us insight only into themselves, and actually obscured the real history of Israel. Form and tradition, however, the pre-literary stages, were where we could really learn something. Again, here we can see the instinctive claim that what is earliest is most authentic, most informative, most true. And we can also see, as with Wellhausen, how the study of the Pentateuch's literary origins is often a pathway to a different goal: the reconstruction of Israel's past, whether religious (Wellhausen), cultural (Gunkel), or social/political (Noth). The text itself is not the endpoint. As a result, it comes to be treated as something of a cipher: the Pentateuch, and indeed the Bible more generally, is understood to encode a truth that only scholarship can retrieve. While this may ostensibly be a second stage, one that follows the source-critical question, it has real effects on the understanding of what the Pentateuch, and its sources, actually are. Are they scripture? Literature? Coded messages about the past? Are they art or history? Are they even interesting, or are the larger literary works merely the framework for the individual episodes? These questions, implicit in the scholarship of the first half of the twentieth century, would become absolutely central in the second half (see the next chapter).

While Gunkel's attention to the pre-literary background of the sources led to the work of Von Rad and Noth, his division of J into two strata, J^a and J^b, would take root in a different line of scholarship. Though P (and D) would remain essentially as described by Wellhausen, the non-priestly sources J and E would be further subdivided, and their literary growth increasingly complicated. The decades following Gunkel would see a proliferation of sources and sigla: J^1 and J^2, L (for "lay" source), K (for "Kenite" source), S (for "Seir" source), N (for "nomadic" source).[6] As the nomenclature suggests, there was little consensus about either the origins or the relative dating of these various materials. Some were understood to precede J and E; some were located between the two; some were later than both. Some were parallel independent sources, some were the basis for J or E, some were dependent on one or the other.

The result was something of a morass of scholarly theories, difficult to wade through. The desire for greater precision in the definition of the non-priestly writings led, instead, to greater confusion. What was once known simply as "J" was now a combination of J^1 and J^2, the latter a conscious expansion of the former; or it was a combination of J and L. E was perhaps independent, or perhaps based on J (with or without L, or J^2, or K, or N). To add to the confusion, now-lost texts were postulated, sources for the sources. Gunkel had already proposed, in passing, that P was based not on J and E but on a work of similarly

6. Respectively: Smend, *Erzählungen*; Eissfeldt, *Old Testament*; Morgenstern, "Oldest Document"; Pfeiffer, "Non-Israelite Source"; Fohrer, *Exodus*.

epic scope (this is how he explained that the late P source could both share some basic features with J and E and yet also contain narratives that are not found in either). Noth had suggested that the similarities between J and E were due to a common underlying source that he termed "G," for *Grundlage*, or "basis" (not to be confused with the "G" that in previous scholarship stood for *Grundschrift*, and was used to denote what is now P). One scholar argued for an even more complicated picture: a G^1 that was the source of a G^2, the latter of which was itself the source for both J and E, while an N source was written as a response to J, but based on G^1. Eventually J and N were combined, then J/N with E.[7]

Despite the variety of specific analyses and sigla, most of these scholars shared the basic conviction that the Pentateuch was the result of gradual growth. Sources may have been independent compositions, but they were understood to be related to and responsive to those that preceded them. As one scholar from this period wrote, "We may reasonably enough, since in any case it fits the majority of the redactions, picture the formation of the Pentateuch as a steady joining on of the younger sources in turn to the older body of material."[8] But how could it be determined what was older and what younger? As might be expected, such judgments were based on the now long-standing notion that the sources can be dated on the basis of their relative theological, cultural, moral, and literary "maturity." A "lay" source must of course be the earliest, as it was identified as being "particularly crude and archaic, . . . the least touched by clerical and cultic interests."[9] How

7. Fohrer, *Überlieferung*.

8. Eissfeldt, *Introduction*, 240.

9. Eissfeldt, *Introduction*, 194.

could a "nomadic" source be anything but early? There is of course some logical circularity at work here: an L or N source that is dated early by virtue of its relative immaturity was isolated and defined in the first place by being relatively immature, and thus early. More to the point, in these scholarly reconstructions the Pentateuch is something of an ongoing project, the earliest sources giving rise to the later. It was already taken as a given that D and P were based on J and E. Here we see attention being given to the question of where J and E might have come from, and the answer is: earlier sources.

Thus even as these scholars worked with theories of written texts, the parallel interest with the pre-literary approaches of Gunkel, Von Rad, and Noth is apparent. All were in pursuit of origins: where did all this material originate? Yet those scholars who proposed further subdivisions of J and E were, in a sense, trying to put old wine into new bottles. No longer were sources identified by their narrative or legal contradictions. Their defining features were now considerably more impressionistic: literary style, or theological profile, or even the topics that they touched on. Yet the theory—written literary sources—that was designed to address the odd literary nature of the Pentateuch was now applied even to texts, J and E, that did not contain those types of contradictions and repetitions. It is almost as if, having learned that identifying sources was the accepted mode of analysis, scholars pursued sources even when the grounds for finding them were no longer present. Or, to put it another way, perhaps somewhat less charitably, scholars after Wellhausen who wanted to work on the question of pentateuchal composition needed something new to say, and as Wellhausen's scheme was relatively simple, the most obvious move was to complicate it.

Indeed, despite the variety of new sources and sigla, all these scholars still shared the basic model inherited from Wellhausen: J and E, however complicated, remained the earliest sources; P remained the latest. Yet, as suggested above, the very attempt to gain further precision achieved much the opposite. As one scholar astutely observed:

> The historical conditions which had brought about these revisions, the purpose for which they had been undertaken, and the nature of the process by which they had been carried through remained, however, undetermined. A growing disagreement inevitably resulted . . . as regards the primary form of the documents themselves, the outlines of which became less and less distinct.[10]

Though virtually no one today talks about J^1 or J^2, or N, L, K, or S, these theories nevertheless had an impact—albeit a negative one.

At the same time that some scholars were adding sources to the picture, others were working in the other direction. We have already seen how J and E, because of Wellhausen's focus on the law, had become increasingly indistinguishable. We have also seen that attempts to divide J and E into even earlier sources obscured the grounds on which they had originally been identified. This trajectory was followed to its logical ends by a pair of German scholars, Paul Volz and Wilhelm Rudolph, who wrote a book entitled "The Elohist as Narrator: An

10. Simpson, *Early Traditions*, 29.

Error of Pentateuchal Criticism?"[11] Focusing on Gen 15–50, they argued, as the title suggests, that there were in fact no grounds for an E source whatsoever.

Their first observation is one that we have already made: that E came into existence in scholarship, with Hupfeld, not on its own recognizance, so to speak, but only through the observation that the older notion of P, the *Grundschrift* or *Urschrift*, could not be a literary unity. The initial step in the analysis of E, in other words, had nothing to do with its independence from J, but only from P. They latched on to the increasingly common statement, found frequently in Wellhausen and those that followed him, that in any given passage J and E, though assumed to be present, were especially difficult to untangle. (Wellhausen, for example, had stated that in the story of the golden calf in Exod 32–34 the separation of J and E was so uncertain that it was best to simply refer to the entirety as "JE" and leave it there.)

Volz and Rudolph also noted that the contemporaneous trend in scholarship to subdivide J and E into three or more early sources—almost the opposite move from that of Wellhausen—resulted in the breaking up of the narrative into ever-smaller units: verses, half-verses, sometimes even individual words. Indeed, when the analysis was undertaken on the grounds of literary style rather than of narrative contradiction and repetition, passages that read perfectly coherently to the naked eye were suddenly fractured. Volz and Rudolph viewed this, not without justification, as the result of a scholarly process of textual disintegration, not a literary process of textual creation. Going back all the way to Astruc, they argued (again, with some justification) that the use of the divine

11. Volz and Rudolph, *Der Elohist*.

names to isolate the sources was faulty. Once that criterion was eliminated, and thus the basic distinguishing characteristic of J and E erased, all of the other lexical and stylistic criteria that followed were equally invalid.

In essence, Volz and Rudolph viewed the features that marked J from E as ticky-tack scholarly nonsense: lexical and stylistic variation is trivial. The stories themselves are clear enough in their literary and theological intention; why should we destroy their meaning on such minor grounds? Yet the narrative contradictions and repetitions remain, and require some sort of explanation. And here they turned to the work of Gunkel and his attention to the oral origins of the written texts. These stories were originally spoken, not written, and—so they argued—repetition and variation are features of oral storytelling: "It is entirely believable that one great storyteller was not in the least afraid to record a story in several variants, to let several ideas flow together into one overarching main idea, to weave together several motifs in a story."[12] What had for so long been the fundamental reason for separating the sources was now, in light of Gunkel's insights, the very reason to keep them together.

While Volz and Rudolph rejected the existence of E as an independent source, they did accept that J might not be a perfect unity. Some of what had been labeled E they allowed might be a later layer of J, or perhaps even a series of unaligned later additions. Their explanation of this was premised on a theory of use: "People wanted to use the magnificent book of stories in lessons and religious services; for this purpose, the work has been reedited, and in this new edition there have been tweaks

12. Volz and Rudolph, *Der Elohist*, 22 (translation mine).

here and there."[13] One can hardly miss the anachronistic imposition of a later scriptural understanding of the Bible onto the history of its composition. For Volz and Rudolph, the Pentateuch is fundamentally a religious text, indeed a text of religious edification. It has been used that way for centuries, and thus must have been so from the beginning, and critical attempts to break it apart thus run counter to the text's own intent.

While we may recognize some of Volz and Rudolph's arguments as inflected by confessional assumptions, we should also give them credit for highlighting both the drawbacks of their contemporaries' theories and the challenge that Gunkel's pre-literary analysis offered to the standard documentary model. What, in the end, were the actual grounds for distinguishing J from E? How does the assumption of oral underpinnings change our understanding of the written sources? It would take a few decades before their criticisms would have an effect on scholarship, but they laid the groundwork for a major overturning of common assumptions.

The first half of the twentieth century in source criticism still belonged to Wellhausen, insofar as everyone was still building on or reacting against him. Yet it is also clear that the notion of a widely accepted compositional history for the Pentateuch is overstated. To use a biblical analogy, Wellhausen's theory was akin to the united monarchy of David and Solomon. Though it is held up as the high point of source criticism, the moment when everything finally coalesced into a unified consensus, it was in fact tenuous at best. Scholarship was varied and messy before Wellhausen. After him, though

13. Volz and Rudolph, *Der Elohist*, 23.

most still held his work in high regard, scholarship was varied and messy again. Some rejected major parts of his work entirely; some, attempting to build on it, only made it more difficult to swallow.

This was a period in which the foundations of the source-critical enterprise, firmly established only a few decades earlier at most, began to totter. They were weighed down from above by increasingly complicated compositional theories, undermined from below by scholars who removed some of their pillars. Affecting everyone was the sudden rise of orality as part of the story. The Pentateuch itself was a different text now: not a combination of coherent sources, but a jumble of pre-literary genres and traditions, a collection of passages and episodes each with its own story to tell.

Some things, however, remained the same. The Romantic mode of biblical criticism endured, to be sure. Earlier materials were both naïve and more authentic, both simple and more trustworthy. The pre-literary shift laid even more emphasis on the notion of literature as the product of the community, the *Volk*. Thus, these stories could tell us something not only about the authors of their written versions but of the spirit and history of the Israelites going back to their very origins. Each literary genre, each tradition, and in fact each written passage, episode, and source could be viewed through the lens of evolution, from naïve to mature, from local to national, from natural to cultic, from lay to theological.

Similarly, the desire to find some sort of truth in the text, a desire that can only be called confessional, persisted (and continues to persist). Moses was no longer the author. The sources themselves were barely authors. But through attentiveness to the smallest units and their postulated pre-literary prehistories, one could still find meaning, history, messages from the past waiting to be decoded in the present. Thus was inaugurated a new phase in source criticism: one that would largely undo the very notion of the sources altogether.

CASE STUDY. GENESIS 28:10–22 (GUNKEL)

In the main, Gunkel, as is to be expected, follows Wellhausen in his source division. As above, J is in plain text, E is in italics, secondary additions are underlined.

> 10 Jacob left Beersheba and went toward Haran. 11 *He came to a certain place and stayed there for the night, because the sun had set. Taking one of the stones of the place, he put it under his head and lay down in that place.* 12 *And he dreamed that there was a stairway set up on the earth, the top of it reaching to heaven, and the angels of God were ascending and descending on it.* 13 And Yahweh stood beside him and said, "I am Yahweh, the God of Abraham your father and the God of Isaac; the land on which you lie I will give to you and to your offspring, 14 and your offspring shall be like the dust of the earth, and you shall spread abroad to the west and to the east and to the north and to the south, and all the families of the earth shall be blessed in you and in your offspring. 15 Know that I am with you and will keep you wherever you go and will bring you back to this land, for I will not leave you until I have done what I have promised you." 16 Then Jacob woke from his sleep and said, "Surely Yahweh is in this place—and I did not know it!" 17 *And he was afraid and said, "How awesome is this place! This is none other than the house of God, and this is the gate of heaven."* 18 *So Jacob*

> *rose early in the morning, and he took the stone that he had put under his head and set it up for a pillar and poured oil on the top of it.* [19]He called that place Bethel, but the name of the city was Luz at the first. [20]*Then Jacob made a vow, saying, "If God will be with me and will keep me in this way that I go and will give me bread to eat and clothing to wear,* [21]*so that I come again to my father's house in peace,* then Yahweh shall be my god, [22]*and this stone, which I have set up for a pillar, shall be God's house, and of all that you give me I will surely give one-tenth to you."*

The most striking departure from Wellhausen is Gunkel's assignment of the entirety of 28:14 to a later hand. This is, however, a wonderful example of Gunkel's approach, as his rationale is entirely grounded in his aesthetic sense of literary style: "This prediction distinguishes itself from the concrete words in vv 13, 15 through its bland attitude and is probably an addition."[14] Narrative continuity, divine names, even terminology are subordinated to literary style.

What distinguishes Gunkel's treatment of these verses from those of his predecessors is not the source division, but rather his discussion of the world behind the text. Behind both J and E is an etiological legend of the founding of a cultic site. The idea of the ladder between heaven and earth that appears in E "is an extremely ancient, originally mythological conception."[15] Gunkel brings parallels not only from Egypt and Mesopotamia, but also from Scandinavia, Germany, and the South Sea islands. Originally, in Gunkel's view, the house of God and gate of heaven would have been not in Bethel but in

14. Gunkel, *Genesis*, 310–11.

15. Gunkel, *Genesis*, 309.

heaven itself; that it appears on earth here is evidence of E "slightly mitigating the mythological elements."[16] Similarly, the anointing of the stone would have once been understood as a sacrifice to the deity who lives within stone itself, but E no longer understood it that way. (Perhaps most remarkable is Gunkel's assertion that the stone that Jacob uses as a pillow and that becomes the basis of the cultic site was immense, and that therefore in the earliest incarnation of this legend Jacob was in fact a giant.)

Gunkel notes the similar wording in Yahweh's promise and Jacob's vow (as we observed in the Hupfeld case study above). Rather than an analytical problem, however, this similarity is now evidence of the common origin of the two stories: "the two recensions of J and E reveal themselves to be fundamentally related"[17]—and note particularly Gunkel's use of the term "recension," signaling that J and E are really just variants of an underlying theme. In particular, Gunkel points to the common ancient assumption that one who migrates to a foreign land wants above all else to return back home.

In keeping with his general approach, Gunkel isolates the elements of the story that he deems "original" and those that are the later innovations of the individual storytellers, J and E. Originally, in his view, on form-critical grounds, this was nothing more than a brief etiology, not even a full narrative: "a brief comment such as those we often encounter as a local tradition," which "explained the sanctity of the stone at Bethel, the origin of the site's name, and the origin of anointing and tithing."[18] This brief account was then set within the broader Jacob

16. Gunkel, *Genesis*, 311.

17. Gunkel, *Genesis*, 313.

18. Gunkel, *Genesis*, 314.

narrative, specifically during Jacob's flight from Esau, and expanded with the promise (J) or vow (E). Moreover, Gunkel claims to be able to distinguish which expanded features are earlier and later: the vow in E is earlier than the promise in J; the direct appearance of the deity in J is earlier than the indirect vision in E. Here we can see how Gunkel's pre-literary analyses don't match up precisely with the source criticism. Both J and E contain earlier and later traditional elements, independent of their literary manifestations. As suggested in this chapter, what we find in this period of scholarship is not just attention to the pre-literary, but also an increasing complexity in the literary analysis. As Gunkel puts it, "We gain insight here, then, into a complicated history."[19]

GUIDING QUESTIONS

1. How did the rise of a concern with the oral or pre-literary affect the analysis of the Pentateuch?
2. What sorts of insights were claimed to be revealed by attention to the pre-literary background of the Pentateuch?
3. How did scholarship of this period complicate Wellhausen's model, and why?

19. Gunkel, *Genesis*, 314.

5

REIMAGINING SOURCE CRITICISM

THOUGH IT WOULD TAKE a few decades, the impact of form and tradition criticism would, beginning in the 1970s, eventually have an impact on the question not only of the pre-literary stages of the Pentateuch's formation but on its literary growth as well. Indeed, it would come to be the defining feature of a major school of source criticism, especially in Germany. In this chapter we will look at the origins and theoretical suppositions of this entirely new approach. For many scholars, this was a period of massive destabilization. The basic scheme of Wellhausen, with its four sources, was suddenly no longer a given. Not only the documentary hypothesis but everything that had been built on it—the religious, cultural, and socio-political history of Israel—was seemingly undermined.

In 1977, the German scholar Rolf Rendtorff published *The Problem of the Process of Transmission in the Pentateuch*, a book in which he laid out a theoretical and methodological argument against not only the pentateuchal sources as classically defined but also the way that scholarship had proceeded in its analysis of the text.[1] The "problem," as Rendtorff defined it, was that traditional source criticism, the documentary hypothesis, was fundamentally incompatible with the form- and tradition-critical conclusions of Gunkel, Von Rad, and Noth. The error that those scholars had made, in his view, was that they had worked entirely within Wellhausen's framework, taking the four sources as their starting point and working backward from them. Yet if their arguments were to be taken seriously, the order needed to be reversed.

As we saw in the previous chapter, one of the main features of both form and tradition criticism was that they took as their primary object of investigation not the final form of the Pentateuch, nor the postulated sources, but rather the episode. It was from the individual episodes that pre-literary genres could be abstracted and underlying traditions could be isolated. It was taken for granted that those episodes had been brought together by collector-authors like J, and so the focus was on how the episodes had originated, rather than how they came together. Rendtorff, however, took for granted the histories of the episodes, and returned focus to their literary growth and combination. "As soon as access to the pentateuchal texts is set in the context of the form-critical method, the statement of the question is basically altered. The Pentateuch as a whole as it lies before is no longer the point of departure, but rather the concrete individual

1. Rendtorff, *Problem*.

text, the 'smallest literary unit.' The work begins as it were at the opposite end."[2]

What is this "smallest literary unit" to which Rendtorff refers? It is the episode, but stripped down in line with form- and tradition-critical analysis. A passage that contains, say, both an etiology and a theological reflection is form-critically mixed; the two elements should be separated. A text that combines, for example, both the Jacob-at-Bethel tradition and the Jacob-and-Esau tradition, which Noth had proposed were originally independent, is likewise a secondary development. The "smallest literary unit" is identified by pulling apart the text until it is in something like a "pure" form. It is only, according to Rendtorff, once we have reduced the Pentateuch to its very building blocks that we can then ask how those were put together. This is the work that, using tradition criticism, Noth had introduced to the field. The independent traditions about Jacob combined into a larger Jacob cycle; that Jacob cycle then combined with the Abraham material (which had its own prehistory), brought together in the larger traditional complex of the patriarchs; that patriarchal complex then combined with that of the exodus and conquest (which, of course, was constructed out of its own set of once-independent traditions). Noth's proposal, in Rendtorff's view, seemingly explained the formation of the Pentateuch without any need for the sources: it is perfectly descriptive of the Pentateuch as we have it.

In that sense, the sources of the documentary hypothesis are not a given, but are rather only one potential way that the smallest literary units could have been assembled. "From the standpoint of the tradition-historical approach, one is justified in accepting continuous

2. Rendtorff, *Problem*, 23.

'sources' in the Péntateuch when, at the end of the tradition-historical inquiry, the source theory offers the most enlightening answer to the questions which arise from the final shape of the text."[3] If, beginning with the smallest literary units, it should happen to be the case that the classical sources emerge naturally as the frameworks into which those units were set, then fine—but to Rendtorff's mind, the documentary hypothesis had failed to make that case. "I cannot at present discern what contribution the documentary hypothesis makes to the question of the formation of the Pentateuch from the smallest units (and their pre-history), across the larger units or the complexes of tradition, to the present synthetic whole."[4]

Unsurprisingly perhaps, to bolster his case Rendtorff pointed to the trends in documentary scholarship we observed in the previous chapter. The splintering of J, in particular, into multiple sources—J^a and J^b, J^1 and J^2, K, L, N—only illustrated the basic lack of strong criteria for the existence of any J at all. "From the time that Wellhausen formulated the now widely accepted documentary hypothesis, there have been distinguished scholars who have constantly supported the division of this oldest pentateuchal source."[5] And the criteria used to bind J together were, in Rendtorff's mind, insufficient. He correctly observed that all too often it was minor word choices, small stylistic features, or loose theological concepts that were offered as defining features. These arguments "show clearly that the exegete, on the basis of the available source hypothesis, seems himself compelled to assign the texts to one of the accepted sources, even

3. Rendtorff, *Problem*, 24.
4. Rendtorff, *Problem*, 173.
5. Rendtorff, *Problem*, 103.

though he has no criteria for doing so."[6] Here Rendtorff may have had Noth in mind, who had suggested that, when in doubt, one should assume that a passage belonged to J. In an overarching sense, Rendtorff saw the continued adherence to the documentary hypothesis, despite the advances of form and tradition criticism, as a sort of scholarly inertia. Though the arguments for it were increasingly tenuous, it was still assumed that the data must be made to fit the traditional model. Rendtorff advocated for starting entirely afresh.

The precise working out of Rendtorff's approach would have to wait for the next generation of scholars, as we will see below. But Rendtorff laid the groundwork for an entirely new direction, that can be boiled down to two main elements, both founded in form and tradition criticism. First, what had, with Gunkel, Von Rad, and Noth, been a pre-literary investigation was transformed into a literary one. No longer were the forms and traditions understood as oral precursors to the written text. They were now the text itself, reducible to the "smallest literary unit," with an emphasis, somewhat ironically, on the word "literary." Where Noth, for example, saw a pre-literary Jacob-at-Bethel tradition, Rendtorff suggested that we should see a Jacob-at-Bethel text, separable from its larger literary context. Second, Rendtorff's model effectively changed the very rationale for the inquiry into the Pentateuch's literary history altogether. It was no longer the literary contradictions and repetitions that drove the need for analysis, but the mere presence in the Pentateuch of independent traditions and their subsequent combination. To put it another way: Rendtorff's theory of the Pentateuch's composition was not dependent on the presence of any literary

6. Rendtorff, *Problem*, 111.

problems, be they narrative, stylistic, lexical, thematic, or theological. Were the Pentateuch to be entirely consistent in these features, it would still be subject to form- and tradition-critical analysis. This was truly a new beginning: what had been the very reason for proposing multiple authors in the Pentateuch, all the way back to Astruc, was no longer particularly relevant.

Much as Wellhausen was the point of departure for the generation of scholars who followed him, Rendtorff would come to be the guiding light for his successors. His approach, and his rejection of the documentary hypothesis, were taken as a given. With very few exceptions, almost every scholar working in the field of pentateuchal criticism for the next quarter century built on Rendtorff's theory. Over time, as we will see, this school of scholarship would go through the same sort of analytical complication as documentary critics had confronted in the first half of the century. But they started with a comparatively simple model, espoused by Rendtorff's student Erhard Blum.[7] It is in Blum's work that we can see Rendtorff's theoretical ideas fleshed out, and thus it is a useful entry into the world of this strand of scholarship.

Blum began (conveniently for our purposes) with the story of Jacob at Bethel in Gen 28:10–22. Noth had identified the core tradition of this episode as an etiology of the cultic site at Bethel—a sort of "George Washington slept here" of ancient Israel. Blum's task was to recover the "smallest literary unit" in the passage: the parts of the text that could have stood together as an independent narrative. The first step, therefore, is one of reduction, the elimination of those elements that are dependent on

7. Blum, *Vätergeschichte* and *Studien.*

or related to other traditions in the Pentateuch—if, after all, the Pentateuch grew by the gradual combination of independent traditions, then those elements that link two once-independent traditions are, almost by definition, secondary. Thus, in our text, the first verse, which moves Jacob from Beersheba to Haran, cannot be part of the original unit, since the rationale for Jacob's flight to Aram comes from the originally distinct Jacob-and-Esau story. Genesis 28:13–15 are also secondary, as they contain a version of the patriarchal promise, which appears across the stories of Abraham, Isaac, and Jacob, and therefore must be understood as a device to link the independent patriarchal stories into a continuous, theologically inflected whole. This promise passage also makes reference to Jacob leaving and returning to the land, again a reference to the Jacob-and-Esau tradition, and thus another indication of a secondary expansion. So too Jacob's speech in the final verses of the passage, which refer to the journey Jacob is taking.

When the elements that refer to or depend on other traditions are excised, what remains is a coherent, simple story: Jacob comes to a certain place, sleeps there, has a dream of divine beings, realizes upon waking that he is in a sacred place, and inaugurates a cultic site there. This, in rough outline, is the original tradition identified by Noth, and the smallest literary unit according to Blum. The next step is to consider how this smallest literary unit grew into its current form. The answer, however, has already basically been announced in the process of whittling down the text to this core form. As Noth had suggested, first the independent Jacob traditions were brought together into a larger Jacob cycle, then the Jacob cycle was combined with those of Abraham and Isaac to form the broader patriarchal complex. And that is precisely what we see here: there are elements that work to bring the Jacob-at-Bethel story together with the Jacob-and-Esau story (the references to Jacob's journey to Haran and his eventual return) and there are elements that connect Jacob with Abraham and Isaac (the patriarchal promise). The textual analysis thus mirrors the tradition-critical, grounding Noth's pre-literary assumptions in the actual words of the Pentateuch.

Even considering only this one passage, we can see how Blum's (and Rendtorff's) approach draws on a range of earlier scholarly theories. Noth is obvious, and openly recognized. So too Von Rad's and Gunkel's idea of J not having been a real author but more of a collector—while Blum doesn't refer to J, he still sees the starting point of the overarching pentateuchal narrative as stemming from the aggregation of previously independent traditions. We may go even further back, however. Pre-literary small independent units were most thoroughly theorized in the first half of the twentieth century, but written small independent texts were postulated by Vater in the first half of the nineteenth century, with the fragmentary hypothesis. The Pentateuch being shaped by theologically minded expansions was the theory of Ewald, also in the nineteenth century, with the supplementary hypothesis. This new approach, then, brought together both the non-documentary models of the distant past and the insights of more recent generations.

The scholarship that followed the path laid down by Rendtorff and Blum is notable for its diversity. While the basic principles of the theory were widely accepted—smaller independent units, secondary links building those units into larger complexes, and the rejection of the classical four-source model—the precise description of the Pentateuch's composition varied significantly from scholar to scholar. In part this was anticipated by Rendtorff, who recognized that when starting from the smallest literary units there were many possibilities for how they might have come together (though his point was that the documents of Wellhausen were not to be assumed). A brief, and necessarily incomplete, look at some of these scholarly possibilities should illustrate the point.

For Blum, the larger traditional complexes, such as the patriarchs and the exodus, existed independently until they were combined into something resembling the overarching pentateuchal narrative by a redactor who worked from what Blum viewed as a deuteronomistic perspective. This text was then supplemented by a second full-scale pentateuchal narrative, this one priestly in orientation (and largely identical with the traditional P source). Blum recognized that this priestly layer had features that were independent of the deuteronomic one, and thus must have had some sort of separate existence, but also suggested that it knew of and was written in order to be a supplement to the existing deuteronomic text. As he put it (in a manner that created some confusion), the priestly material was "neither source nor redaction."[8]

Other scholars concluded that there was in fact no connection between the patriarchal and exodus complexes, and thus no overarching pentateuchal narrative, before the priestly text. Thus Blum's pre-priestly deuteronomic composition was rejected, replaced by the idea that the non-priestly texts that explicitly link the non-priestly patriarchal and exodus materials must, in

8. Blum, *Studien*, 229 (translation mine).

fact, be post-priestly, since they build on the new priestly continuous story. (Blum would come to agree with this position in later publications.) Another theory held that the pentateuchal narrative was the creation of a figure called "J"—though not the same J of the documentary hypothesis. This J was, in the style of Von Rad, a collector and theological editor. Every individual episode could be broken down into the early fragments that preceded J, the contributions of J himself, and a series of post-J additions. There are, in addition, multiple layers of J, which in aggregate result in the complete non-priestly text of the Pentateuch, to which P was added.

A number of scholars from this school of thought produced studies of the individual pentateuchal books, each of which offered a slightly different version of the theory. Perhaps the greatest variation can be seen in the analysis of individual episodes, those smallest literary units. While Blum had kept it relatively simple, essentially following the outline provided by Noth, the approach lends itself to a certain openness and flexibility that allows for widely divergent treatments of the same text. What constitutes the original core, and what is supplementary? The answers depend largely on the preferences and predispositions of the scholar. As an example we may consider the story of Jacob tricking Isaac into giving him Esau's blessing, from Gen 27. What is the core of this story, and what is a later addition? According to one scholar (and here I am aware that I am drawing from a relatively extreme example), Rebekah was not originally part of the tradition, so everything to do with her is one additional layer. The first conversation in the story between Isaac and Jacob is later still, as it links back to the story of Isaac tricking Esau in Gen 25. A subsequent layer can be found in all the parts of the passage that emphasize the blessing, a theme that extends throughout Genesis and even into Numbers. Also secondary are the identification of Esau with Edom, which is connected with Gen 25; perceived allusions to Judah's primacy over Edom; the prophecy of Edom's eventual independence from Judah; and the etymology of Jacob's name. All of these, it should be noted, are understood to be separate and sequential redactional interventions. Finally, the last verse of the chapter, which connects back to the priestly material in Gen 26 and 28, was added. But not quite finally—there are also a couple of what are termed, confusingly, "post-redactional" additions, which add seemingly banal details: the identification of Esau's gear as his quiver and bow, and the description of Esau's clothes.[9]

I offer this lengthy (yet abbreviated) summary to point out that while extreme, perhaps, this analysis merely drinks very deeply of the Rendtorff well. Even the very first proposed layer raises the question: how does one separate addition from tradition? On what grounds does one decide whether Rebekah was part of the "smallest literary unit" or not? As I have suggested, while the basic theory may be widely accepted, its practical application is mostly uncontrolled. This scholar found ten layers in Gen 27; others, working from the same perspective, find five, or four, or, in the case of Blum, only one. This can be repeated with many passages in the Pentateuch.

As an additional layer of complication, there is a significant cluster of scholars who consider the original combination of the priestly and non-priestly texts, however defined, to have resulted not in a Pentateuch, but in a Hexateuch—that is, a work encompassing what is now

9. Levin, *Der Jahwist*, 207–15.

Genesis through Joshua—or even an Octateuch or Enneateuch (extending through Samuel or Kings). The Pentateuch, in this view, was actually a (still) later edition of this larger work. As a result, there are traces to be found in the text not only of the redaction of the non-priestly materials and of the combination of those with the priestly, but also of the redactor who created the Hexateuch, and of the redactor who created the Pentateuch. Thus, it is not only the identity of the smallest literary units that is up for debate, but also of the much larger literary units. Even the Pentateuch itself no longer holds its shape.

It is perhaps a feature of pentateuchal criticism—or maybe of biblical scholarship more generally—that what is posited as a relatively simple theory is made increasingly complicated by subsequent studies. We have seen it already with the generations following Wellhausen, and it is true also of those following Rendtorff. What was revolutionary in Blum's early work came to seem rather benign in light of what would follow. Where one scholar sees five layers, the next finds six. The flexibility of the theory makes this possible; the natural desire to say something distinctive from one's scholarly predecessors makes it almost inevitable.

While it may have become clear from the preceding discussion, it should be stated clearly that the bulk of the novelty in Rendtorff's theory, and those who followed him, is related to the non-priestly material, what had previously been identified as J and E. Yet while the texts that are recognizably priestly had been largely agreed on since the nineteenth century, the nature of those texts, and of P as a whole, underwent significant changes, and it is worth treating those briefly here.

Perhaps the primary question about the priestly material is whether it is to be understood as an independent source or as a redactional layer. Both options are put forward by those following Rendtorff, though in different configurations. For some, P is simply another layer grafted on to, and dependent on, the non-priestly text(s). For others, it is quasi-independent: written originally to stand alone, but nevertheless based on and responding to the earlier non-priestly material. (This is not so far from Wellhausen's view.) Blum, as we have seen, tries to thread the needle between these two possibilities: neither source nor redaction. Some propose that P was indeed truly independent, built on an unrecoverable body of tradition, and perhaps constructed, like the non-priestly material, out of previously independent small literary units (e.g., narratives, genealogies, ritual instructions).

The increasingly common position that P was the first writing to bring together the patriarchal and exodus traditions, as noted above, has led to a concomitant increase in attention to what are described as "post-priestly" texts. For some scholars, this body of material includes a significant portion of what were once assigned to J and E. Thus, for example, while the basic separation of the flood story into two hands has remained relatively stable for nearly three centuries, there are those now who claim that the P story is the original one, while the non-priestly flood story is a later expansion of it. There is disagreement, of course, about the extent of this post-priestly reworking.

There is also an ongoing question about the scope of P, especially in its purported original form. Since the late nineteenth century, it had been commonly understood that P extended all the way through the Pentateuch. More recently, some scholars have suggested that in fact

P originally ended much earlier (though, unsurprisingly, precisely where is up for debate). Some set the ending as early as Exod 29, with the instructions for building the tabernacle; some extend it through the end of Exodus, with the construction of the tabernacle; others take it further still. Many share the opinion that the earliest version of P contained only narrative, and that the ritual-legal material is a much later addition. P is sometimes broken up into three distinct sections: the narrative of Genesis and Exodus, the legal-ritual material of Leviticus, and then the yet later mixed narrative and legal content of Numbers. Whether all of this should still bear the label "P" is unclear, as what is priestly sometimes precedes the non-priestly, and sometimes comes after it. Sometimes it exists independently of the non-priestly, and sometimes it depends on it, or even on the combination of the non-priestly and an earlier stage of the priestly writings.

Though the variety of opinions is, typically, quite wide, the simple recognition that the priestly writings in the Pentateuch are not a unity is an old and common one. Already in the late nineteenth century it was observed that the bulk of Lev 17–26 seems to have a different character from the rest of P. These chapters were labeled the "Holiness" laws, because they contain the refrain "You shall be holy for I, Yahweh your God, am holy." But as with so much in pentateuchal scholarship, this observation would undergo dramatic shifts. At first it was assumed that the Holiness material, commonly abbreviated as H, was the earliest part of P. This was because it was assumed—in the grand Romantic (or antisemitic) tradition of the period—that these laws, which are unusually attentive to moral and ethical behavior, must have been earlier than the more cultic and ritually-oriented laws in the first half of Leviticus. It would not be until the late twentieth century that virtually the entire field came to the recognition that in fact H was a later layer of P, dependent on the ritual laws but broadening their relatively narrow scope. Thus the basic idea that P might be multilayered is hardly new. In fact, some scholars still working with a documentary idea of P argued that H was not only a layer of P, but was even a redactional layer of the entire Pentateuch, and could be found in passages outside of Lev 17–26.

Most of the scholars working with Rendtorff's model, however, have rejected the label "H" altogether, in part, it seems, because H presumes P, and P itself is no longer a consistent concept. What generally belongs to the priestly writings is still relatively constant. But what those texts are, how they came to be, and how they relate to each other and to the rest of the Pentateuch is undergoing the same sort of destabilization that befell J and E.

In the nearly half century since Rendtorff published his book, the field of source criticism has undergone a near-total revolution. Today, virtually the entirety of continental European scholarship is working with Rendtorff's model, and a number of scholars elsewhere as well. With the variation among individual scholars, it is nearly impossible to describe all the specific compositional theories. For the lay reader, student, or non-specialist, it is thus sometimes difficult to find one's footing in this area. How to make sense of the pre-priestly, priestly, and post-priestly scheme? What is the import of Tetrateuch, Hexateuch, and Pentateuch? How many layers are in any given passage, and how to adjudicate between various competing arguments? Though the trees are thick, the forest is nevertheless recognizable. We can thus step back and consider some of the underlying ideas and effects.

As noted above, the foundations of this approach can be found in the form and tradition criticisms that developed at the beginning of the twentieth century. In one sense, what we see here are these modes taken to their logical conclusions. If, in fact, the pentateuchal narrative is really the product of the combination of once-independent traditions that have been brought together into larger complexes, as Noth argued, then here is that idea worked through without the assumption of the classical pentateuchal documents.

Yet at the same time Rendtorff's ideas undercut what was perhaps the basic insight of form and tradition criticism, at least as they were originally intended. Gunkel's fundamental claim was that the biblical text was rooted in oral communication, in pre-literary traditions. In shifting from the abstracted pre-literary genre or tradition to the "smallest literary unit," Rendtorff and those who followed him have largely done away with the idea of orality altogether. In one sense, there is a logic to this: as some have pointed out, we have no access to the oral—what we have is what is on the page, and compositional theories that rely on a notion of orality are therefore built on shaky ground. On the other hand, it seems vanishingly unlikely that there were no shared pre-literary (or even extra-literary) traditions in ancient Israel, and compositional theories that don't even allow for common stories or concepts suffer perhaps from a lack of cultural realism.

The move from pre-literary tradition to text also raises questions of materiality. Very small stories are relatively understandable in an oral context. But when we talk about the "smallest literary unit," and we point to the actual words in the Bible and say "this is the original text of this story," we are claiming that this handful of verses (in the case of the Jacob-at-Bethel story, for example) existed not just as an independent literary unit but as an independent material text. This is somewhat hard to swallow: we are forced to imagine an ancient Israel in which stories were not told and shared orally, but were written down a paragraph here and a paragraph there, floating in space until someone thought to bring them together.

The oral has been (re-)replaced by the written. Or, to put it another way, orality has been replaced by scribalism. The inaccessible, if conceivable, oral transmission of traditions is understood in this model to be rather the manifestly accessible work of ancient Israel's elite literary professionals. In this way the cultural reach of the text is reduced. We are dealing no longer with common Israel-wide culture and traditions, but only with the virtually closed community of trained scribes. Though we have little to no evidence, biblical or otherwise, for how scribes worked in Israel, there is extensive comparative material from elsewhere in the ancient Near East, especially in Mesopotamia. There we see, in a manner similar to that proposed by pentateuchal scholars, older texts being copied and recopied, edited and expanded, all within the scribal schools, often even as part of the scribal educational curriculum.

One common feature of this approach is the relatively late dating of much of the pentateuchal material. As we have seen, the idea of the late priestly writings has survived from Wellhausen. When much of the non-priestly text is increasingly assigned to a post-priestly layer, this means that the chronological center of the whole is quite late indeed. Here again the analyses of

Gunkel and Noth, though taken as a conceptual basis, are overthrown. Form and tradition criticism were a way of accessing the earliest stages of Israel's culture and history, a way of getting beyond and behind the text. When there is nothing but the text, nothing beyond or behind it, the historical possibilities, tentative though they may have been, are foreclosed.

What remains, however, is—again, and again unsurprisingly—the Romantic notion of development and evolution. It is taken for granted that the history of the text is a transition from short to long, from simple to complex, from local to national. It is assumed that later texts are more concerned with morals, ethics, theology, cult, priesthood. Wellhausen's literary reconstruction may have been rejected, but his underlying assumptions remain in good standing.

Similarly maintained is Wellhausen's claim (building on those before him) that what the biblical texts provide is not information about the periods they describe but about the periods in which the text were written. Ironically, it was this very claim that Gunkel and Noth attempted to move past, finding in the pre-literary backgrounds of the texts insight into the time before they were written. When the pre-literary is merged with the literary, the texts once again are grounded only in the time of their composition. Now, however, it is not the pentateuchal documents that speak to their compositional contexts, but the smallest literary units—and every layer and larger complex that follows from them. Each story, each layer, each stage of development is assumed to stem from a specific, and identifiable, cultural or historical moment. What's more, each story, layer, and stage is read as if its literary purpose is in fact to tell the reader about that cultural or historical moment. The text becomes something of a code to be broken: what is this text "really" about?

The most observable innovation in this approach is the replacement of independent sources with a series of layers, each building on the previous. What is maybe not so obvious is what such an approach says about the nature of the Pentateuch. From the moment that the first major blocks of material were created, there was a main text. It was not a Pentateuch, perhaps, but a piece of writing that existed in ancient Israel that, to the presumed exclusion of all others, told this story. Each layer of that text changed its perspective somewhat, but the text remained—not just the idea of it, but literally the text itself. We can get back to the "smallest literary unit" because it is still visible, preserved as if in amber. Moreover, it is assumed that the purpose of each new layer was, at least to its contemporary audience, recognizable. A reader of the newly enlarged whole would be able to tell what was older and passé, and what was new and authoritative. (It is, of course, not clear how a reader would in fact be able to do this. Given, say, the flood story with its two purported layers, how could one know which is meant to override the other?)

There are two conceptual outcomes here. First, the Pentateuch has, in some form, existed as a continuously authoritative text from its very origins. Whether this authority is understood in a broader cultural sense is unclear, since it is generally assumed that most Israelites would have had no idea of what was actually in the text. But in a narrow sense—given the assumption that all of the literary activity was taking place in this one text, over and over again—there is some textual authority at work here. Second, at each stage of its redaction, with each layer that was added to it, the "meaning" of the Pentateuch was always clear. There was no point at which, say, four independent texts were jumbled together into a haphazard and literarily confusing whole. Rather, every moment of the text's development can be explained as a conscious, often theological, effort at updating and revising in light of changed cultural and historical circumstances. As observed above, in this approach the contradictions and duplications cease to matter much. The text thus makes sense, makes meaning, in a new way with every new layer, and once we can discern those layers, and those meanings, we can see how the Pentateuch was in fact always coherent. There is, of course, nothing necessarily wrong with either of these positions. But they are, individually and especially taken together, rather strikingly Protestant in their formulation. It is sola scriptura and ad fontes wrapped into one theoretical package.

CASE STUDY. GENESIS 28:10–22 (BLUM)

We have already had the opportunity to discuss Blum's approach to our case study text above, but here we can see the text with its various layers laid out. The original "smallest literary unit" is in plain text; material attributable to the Jacob cycle is in italics; additions associated with the creation of the patriarchal complex are underlined; and the text that belongs to Blum's deuteronomistic composition layer is double underlined.

> 10 <u>Jacob left Beersheba and went toward Haran</u>.
> 11 He came to a certain place and stayed there
> for the night, because the sun had set. Taking
> one of the stones of the place, he put it under
> his head and lay down in that place.
> 12 And he
> dreamed that there was a stairway set up on
> the earth, the top of it reaching to heaven, and

> the angels of God were ascending and descending on it. [13]And Yahweh stood beside him and said, "I am Yahweh, the God of Abraham your father and the God of Isaac; the land on which you lie I will give to you and to your offspring, [14]and your offspring shall be like the dust of the earth, and you shall spread abroad to the west and to the east and to the north and to the south, and all the families of the earth shall be blessed in you and in your offspring. [15]Know that I am with you and will keep you wherever you go and will bring you back to this land, for I will not leave you until I have done what I have promised you." [16]Then Jacob woke from his sleep and said, "Surely Yahweh is in this place—and I did not know it!" [17]And he was afraid and said, "How awesome is this place! This is none other than the house of God, and this is the gate of heaven." [18]So Jacob rose early in the morning, and he took the stone that he had put under his head and set it up for a pillar and poured oil on the top of it. [19]He called that place Bethel, but the name of the city was Luz at the first. [20]*Then Jacob made a vow, saying, "If God will be with me and will keep me in this way that I go and will give me bread to eat and clothing to wear,* [21]*so that I come again to my father's house in peace,* then Yahweh shall be my god, [22]*and this stone, which I have set up for a pillar, shall be God's house, and of all that you give me I will surely give one-tenth to you."*

As described above, the first step in Blum's analysis is the removal from the story of those elements that are clearly dependent on other narratives. Thus 28:10, which places Jacob's family in Beersheba (a reference to Gen 26:23), and which has Jacob heading toward Haran (Gen

27:43) is eliminated from the core text. Genesis 28:15, with its mention of Jacob's flight and eventual return, is dependent on the narrative of Gen 27; so too the vow in 28:20–22. These are also removed. The self-introduction of Yahweh in 28:13 presumes the genealogical connection of the three patriarchs Abraham, Isaac, and Jacob, while the promise found in 28:13–14 is closely related to those given to Abraham in Gen 13:14–16 and 12:3. These verses too are thus not original to the independent Bethel tradition.

Building up from the core narrative, then, the earliest independent Bethel tradition can be isolated in 28:11–12, the first clause of 28:13, and 28:16–19. This was an etiology of the sanctuary at Bethel, linked to the figure of the ancestor Jacob. At this stage, the other two major Jacob texts/traditions were also independent: Jacob and Esau on one hand, Jacob and Laban on the other. These three Jacob elements were brought together into a larger Jacob cycle by the insertion of the vow in 28:20–22. The Jacob cycle, in turn, was combined with the Abraham-Isaac material to form the overarching patriarchal narrative. In our passage, 28:13–14 do this work, with the patriarchal promise, which spans all three generations. Also belonging to this stratum is 28:10, which takes Jacob's destination from the Jacob cycle (Gen 27) but his origin from the Isaac cycle (Gen 26). Finally, the patriarchal complex was combined with the other major blocks of tradition by an author/editor with the full scope of the narrative in view, extending not just to the end of the Pentateuch but through Joshua as well. To this deuteronomistic layer belong 28:15 and the end of 28:21, which Blum sees as picking up on elements from the patriarchal complex but inflecting them with language and ideology from this later stage of development.

As noted above, this approach is more concerned with the isolation of literary units and the manner in which they might have grown and been combined than it is with the traditional issues of source criticism. Notably, Blum's core narrative preserves two of the main internal inconsistencies that drove previous analyses: the double appearance of the angels (28:12) and Yahweh (28:13), and the double reaction of Jacob (28:16 and 28:17). While the divine names are not a concern for Blum, other linguistic and stylistic elements are central to his argument, especially in his identification of deuteronomistic features.

The result of all this is a narrative that can be read in each of its various stages and contexts. The core narrative stands alone; the next stage can be read along with the rest of the Jacob cycle; the next stage with the entire patriarchal complex; and the last with essentially the entire non-priestly Pentateuch. That is, the passage always remains coherent within each successive context.

GUIDING QUESTIONS

1. What is the relationship between the oral and the written in Rendtorff's approach?
2. How does the process of starting from "the smallest literary unit" compare with previous analyses of the Pentateuch?
3. What are the benefits and drawbacks of Rendtorff's model?

6

A RETURN TO THE SOURCES

ALTHOUGH RENDTORFF'S APPROACH HAS become dominant in much of pentateuchal scholarship, especially in continental Europe, an alternative model has continued to exist, and has gained in popularity, especially in the United States. It is not an entirely new compositional theory—it is, in fact, quite old at its roots—but it has gained new life through a focus on method and analytical clarity. It is, in brief, a return to the classical sources: J, E, P, and D. But the means by which these sources are identified, how they were combined, and how they relate to each other are all rethought and presented afresh. In this final chapter we will look at this approach, which has come to be known as the "neo-documentary hypothesis."

At first blush, the neo-documentary hypothesis may appear to be a backlash against the rise of the fragmentary/supplementary model of Rendtorff. In fact, it originated more as a response to the same kinds of complicated documentary models that Rendtorff himself was also reacting to. Its roots can be traced to Israeli scholarship of the 1980s, in particular Menahem Haran. Haran, however, never fully published his ideas, leaving them instead to his teaching and a few illuminating footnotes scattered throughout his writings. Baruch Schwartz, a student of Haran, took it one step further, in articles and conference presentations, and again especially in his teaching of students. Schwartz, unlike Haran, worked at a time when the documentary theory was already being eclipsed in many parts of the field, and therefore responded more directly to Rendtorff and his school. It was one of Schwartz's students—full disclosure: it's me—who gave the theory a full treatment, in a number of books and articles, foremost among them *The Composition of the Pentateuch: Renewing the Documentary Hypothesis*.[1] Others taught or influenced by Schwartz have also published studies that expound or rely on this renewed approach, including prominently Jeffrey Stackert.

Like Rendtorff, the neo-documentary approach recognizes that scholarship of the first half of the twentieth century produced rather unwieldy results. The proliferation of sources and sub-sources, and with them the increasingly splintered nature of the text, held increasingly less explanatory power. Attempts to get back beyond the text, with form and tradition criticism, had almost unavoidably affected the analysis of the text itself (as would become abundantly clear in the work of Rendtorff et al.). What had been lost, seemingly, was the original underlying rationale for undertaking any of this work: the confused state of the Pentateuch as we have it.

1. Baden, *Composition.*

What makes the Pentateuch unique is not that it is form-critically mixed, nor that a wide range of presumably once-independent traditions can be identified in it. This is true of virtually all biblical literature, and in fact most literature, full stop. The shifting literary styles, or the alternating uses of terms, even of the names and titles of the deity, while a point of curiosity, are also not the main issues in the text. The canonical flood story, to take a famous example, is difficult to read not because it contains prose and poetry and building instructions and blessings, all distinct form-critical elements. It is difficult not because it contains both a core narrative of the flood as well as links to other putatively independent traditions, like the Cain and Abel story in Gen 4 or the so-called Table of Nations in Gen 10. It is difficult not because it uses both "Yahweh" and "Elohim" for the deity, or because it contains two terms for "dry land," or two words for "perish." It is difficult—and so for the entirety of the Pentateuch—because it is incoherent as a story, on the very basic level of the plot. Not what words or style or tradition or genres are used, but what is actually happening—how many animals? how long did the flood last? what bird?—this is what makes the text problematic. And if the problem is one of narrative, then the solution, in the view of the neo-documentary hypothesis, should also be one of narrative.

Methodologically, this is a response to most of twentieth-century scholarship. On the source side, it is a rejection of the increasing reliance on style and terminology to pick texts apart, a trend that saw ostensibly perfectly readable stories chopped into unreadable pieces. It is also a reminder that the object of study is, contra Rendtorff, in fact the canonical text, the Pentateuch as a whole, rather than the forms, traditions, or smallest literary units therein. It seeks neither to create problems where none appear, nor to ignore the problems that are evident on the surface of the text.

In practical terms, the neo-documentary approach is relatively simple. Narrative claims that cannot be part of the same story are separated; those that must be part of the same story are connected. The first step, on its own, forms the basis of both source and fragmentary theories. It is the second step that distinguishes the neo-documentary theory (and the classical source criticism of previous generations) from the newer supplementary model. Those elements that connect passages are seen not as secondary links, but as an inherent part of the text. Cross-references are narrative devices, not merely editorial ones. When, in Gen 28, we find repeated allusions to Jacob fleeing from Esau, those are indications that the two episodes belong to the same story. Internal coherence within stories, and sources, is most highly prized.

The neo-documentary hypothesis does not begin with a presupposition of the four classical sources. It begins, rather, with the canonical text, and with the two basic steps described above. The four sources are the result of the analysis, not its starting point. When the contradictory elements are separated, and the consistent elements linked, it turns out that four major strands emerge. The contrast with Rendtorff should be clear. It is true enough that starting from the "smallest literary units" may not result in the four sources of classical scholarship. But the neo-documentary hypothesis does not start from those smaller units. It starts from the received text. When the literary problem of the Pentateuch is its contradictions, rather than the question of where all these stories came from, the answer is the simplest mode of resolving those contradictions.

In another sharp turn away from both Rendtorff and the later developments of the classical documentary model, the neo-documentary hypothesis takes a pared-down view of the manner in which the Pentateuch was redacted. As we saw above, source critics of the twentieth century devised increasingly complicated theories of redaction, involving multiple steps of combination (J^1 + J^2, J + E, JE + D, JED + P, etc.), each step requiring not only a redaction, but also a definable mode of redaction, identifiable redactional elements in the text, and more. Those working with the Rendtorff model have, as we have seen, dramatically expanded the number of redactions and their import. Passages are understood to be the product of repeated redactional intervention, each reshaping the text anew, each to be isolated and explained.

From the neo-documentary perspective, however, the redaction of the text is, for the most part, little more than the necessary by-product of the existence of the sources. If the Pentateuch is a combination of multiple documents, then they must have been combined. Anything that we might say about that process must be derived from the textual evidence. We can say, therefore, that the documents were combined with an eye toward preservation, despite the resulting contradictions. Virtually no attempt was made to smooth out the rough edges created when the sources were put together—otherwise we wouldn't have the very contradictions on the basis of which the sources are identifiable and the Pentateuch is problematic. The sources were, of course, arranged in a basic chronological order—our Pentateuch doesn't ever jump backward from Jacob to Abraham, or from the wilderness to Egypt. Thus the creation of a chronological coherence, if not a coherence in the details of the plot, must have been a priority (and sensibly enough). Beyond that, however, there is relatively little to be said.

Perhaps most strikingly, the neo-documentary hypothesis posits, in the simplest terms, a single redaction for all four sources. This is less a matter of positive proof and more one of an absence of counter-evidence. To claim that J and E were brought together into a combined "JE" before their combination with any other sources, for example, requires some textual signs that the manner in which J and E were interwoven is different from how J and P, or P and E, or J and D were combined. For neo-documentary scholars, no such signs exist. That is, the redactional method seems to be the same from Gen 1 through the end of Deuteronomy, across all the books and all the sources, regardless of which happen to be present in any given passage. Furthermore, this redaction—in sharp opposition to the Rendtorff model—has imprinted the text with no overarching ideology. For this reason, many neo-documentary scholars use the term "compiler" or "compilation," to highlight the sole identifiable function of the redaction: the bringing together of the documents.

In a sense, the neo-documentary hypothesis requires little detailed explanation. Four sources, one redaction. This is, of course, an oversimplification, even if it remains the basic structure of the argument. The neo-documentary hypothesis posits that the four sources were each independent documents before their combination. This independence, however, refers only to their existence as stand-alone texts. D, it is argued, knew of both J and E, and built on them, at times borrowing from them nearly verbatim. Yet, contrary to the opinion commonly held since Wellhausen, D did not know a combined J and E. In D's telling of the Israelites' encounter with the deity at the mountain in the wilderness, for example, it follows the E storyline nearly point for point. But in Exodus, E's story is closely interwoven with J's version of the same event. For D to use only the E material indicates that either D was reading an independent E, or that D was—improbably—the first source critic, and the only one for over two thousand years.

Likewise, while neo-documentary scholars generally assert that P was written without any knowledge of the other sources, this is true only of the basic layer of the priestly source. The H stratum—which is understood to be a secondary layer of P—seems to have been aware of, and in fact responded directly to, D. Nevertheless, P (with H) existed on its own. That is to say, although D may have known E and J, and H may have known D, none of the documents was written in order to be a supplement to anything that preceded it. Each was written to be read independently. This is essentially a return to the position of Hupfeld, who, as we saw above, had argued that none of the sources could also have served as a redactor (or as a supplement), because the combination of the documents inevitably leads to the distorting, in the combined text, of their internally consistent positions. The neo-documentary hypothesis allows for relationships among the documents—though fewer than previous scholarship held—but also for their literary, or perhaps better, conceptual and material, independence.

It also returns to the ideas of Gunkel and Noth, largely in their original formulation, not as the main focus of the theory but as a dependent corollary. One of the reasons that J, E, and P are considered to have been unaware of each other is that while they share much of the same macrostructure, and even some of the same individual episodes, they tell their stories in very different ways, with different details, characters, places, and timings. J thinks that the flood lasted forty days; P thinks it lasted 150. If P knew the flood story only from reading J (or vice versa, theoretically), where did it get the number 150 from? Why did it think it was a raven rather than a dove that Noah sent from the ark? These differences—especially the minor ones—speak to an independent version of the story. And yet: it is still the same story. Both J and P have Abraham separating from Lot; both J and E have Joseph being taken by force to Egypt; both E and P have Jacob's name being changed to Israel. Common Israelite oral traditions—whether we accept the cultural and social/political histories that Gunkel and Noth attached to them—have strong explanatory power in this regard. (They also explain how story elements in the Pentateuch are found outside of it—as in, for example, the identification of Jacob and Israel in multiple psalms—without supposing that one text must have been familiar with another, in either direction.)

In terms of redaction, here too the simplicity of the basic model is more complex upon closer examination. As noted above, the existence of contradictions in the canonical Pentateuch is evidence that the redaction was broadly preservationist, attempting to keep as much of the original source material as possible. Yet the creation of a chronologically consistent final product was, it is suggested, at times at odds with the presentation in the independent documents. For example: in J, Isaac (almost certainly) died upon giving his children his deathbed blessing, in

Gen 27, before Jacob fled to Aram. In P, however, Isaac dies only after Jacob returns from Aram, and is buried by his two sons, Jacob and Esau, together, at the end of Gen 35. Isaac can hardly die twice, of course—and so the announcement of his death in Gen 27 has been excised from the text (resulting in the bizarre circumstance of Isaac seemingly being on his deathbed for over twenty years). Similarly, in J manna was provided to the Israelites at the beginning of their journey in the wilderness, in Exod 16; according to P, this happened after the Israelites had left Sinai, in the middle of what is now Numbers. As the Israelites could hardly receive the manna for the first time twice, the P story has been relocated, interwoven with the J material back in Exodus (and resulting in some strange anachronisms). The redactional process may, in the neo-documentary model, be substantially simpler than in previous scholarship, but it is not simplistic.

In its focus on the four documents and the moment of their redaction, the neo-documentary hypothesis can sometimes seem to artificially minimize the entire literary history of the Pentateuch, in a way that seems not to take into account the way that texts are usually understood to have been created and transmitted in the ancient world. Neo-documentary scholars often—and I am certainly guilty of this—conflate the documents with authors, using "J" to refer to both the text and its writer, or describe the process of redaction by reference to the figure of the redactor and what he must have been intending. This is, however, most likely anachronistic. The idea of the author as an individual genius is a relatively modern one, and certainly not at home in the ancient Near East, where virtually no texts are attributed to an individual by name. Although we may not have access to the precise way that scribes worked in ancient Israel, we can certainly say that the Pentateuch, like every written text that we have, is a scribal product. We should, therefore, be thinking not about the one person who sat down and wrote J, or P, nor necessarily the one person who put them together. Rather, the picture should more be one of schools—if not actual scribal schools, then at least schools of thought—that are responsible for the production of these texts. And, moreover, we should be thinking about schools that existed over time, over multiple generations, and thus also about texts that existed, and changed, over time.

That is to say: even while neo-documentary scholars talk about the theoretically single moment when the four sources were combined, this is not the end (or the beginning) of the story of the Pentateuch's literary history. That moment of combination may have been responsible for the main shape of the text, but it does not account for every word of it. Increasingly neo-documentary scholarship has paid attention to the presence in the text of secondary, post-redaction, additions. As may be expected, there are relatively fewer such additions in this model than there are in other scholarly approaches. But there are still likely dozens of passages, smaller or larger, that show signs of having been added to the Pentateuch after the sources were brought together. The most easily recognizable of these are identifiable because they break the rules of the model. Even when two sources have been combined in a passage, they are generally separable because their individual characteristics have been maintained in the process of redaction. Yet there are some passages where elements from multiple sources are present in an inseparable way. The covenant and laws given to Moses in Exod 34:10–27, for example, show clear dependence on and borrowing from texts belonging to E, P, and D, but are presented as a coherent literary unit. There are also passages where a loose element recognizable from one source appears in an otherwise self-contained block of another source. Thus, for instance, the character of Miriam is known in the Pentateuch only in E—no one else mentions her—yet in one of the P census lists, in Num 26, we read that Amram bore Aaron and Moses "and their sister Miriam." That final phrase appears to be a secondary addition, one that, with knowledge of the canonical story, filled out the genealogy to match.

There is, of course, an element of circularity at work here. The sources are defined as having certain features, and when a text is encountered that seems to challenge those definitions, it is simply marked as a later addition. This is, perhaps, not so different from what we saw with Rendtorff et al., where the smallest literary units are isolated and everything that doesn't fit is declared to be secondary. The neo-documentary defense would be that as a percentage of the whole these later additions are very small. The sources are defined not by some a priori notion of what they should say, but by the inductive analysis of the text that we have. It is only after the contours of the sources and the stories that they tell have emerged that those (relatively rare) elements that do not fit begin to stick out. At the same time, this is one of the ways that neo-documentary scholarship allows for the inevitable ongoing growth of the pentateuchal text. It is not imagined that, once the documents were combined, the Pentateuch suddenly achieved some sort of sacred and unchangeable status. Rather, like any text, it was passed down, and adjusted in ways large and small by a series of readers, or scribes, who sought to correct, expand, and otherwise edit it. In this sense, it is something of a miracle that we can still recognize the sources as clearly as we can.

What is true of the combined Pentateuch is true also of its constituent parts, the sources. There is no reason to think—indeed, there is good reason not to think—that the source documents were perfectly stable from the moment they were composed until the moment they were combined with each other. We have already noted that it is widely accepted by scholars of every stripe that the priestly writing has gone through multiple rounds of editing: P, and H, and, most scholars would hold, post-H layers as well. D is also commonly acknowledged to contain earlier and later strata (though the details may vary from scholar to scholar). And while the evidence is less obvious, perhaps, the same is almost certainly true for J and E as well, and scholars have begun to identify some of these passages. The neo-documentary hypothesis, as a compositional theory, may focus on one specific moment in the Pentateuch's literary history, but it does not claim that to be the first, last, or only moment.

The analytical distinctiveness of the neo-documentary hypothesis, as opposed to both the classical documentary model of Wellhausen and his successors or the new approach of Rendtorff and those that followed him, should be clear. What remains is to think about some of the deeper issues that are at stake. Foremost among these is the rejection of the Romantic evolutionary scheme that has been a nearly constant feature of pentateuchal scholarship for the past two centuries. Although the neo-documentary model does recognize some relative chronology among the sources—D after J and E, H after D—it does not suggest that what we are seeing in the text is to be understood as evidence for broad cultural or ideological development. Importantly, although D, for example, may have been written in light of J and E, all three sources continued to exist independently, and thus continued to be relevant to some segment of the living Israelite community, contemporaneously. Rather than stand as evidence of change, they are evidence of diversity. One school of thought in ancient Israel may have held to the priestly understanding at the same time that another held to the deuteronomic. The Romantic attachment to the earlier material as more natural and authentic, and the later as derivative and decadent, is entirely absent.

Equally rejected, therefore, is the common notion that the sources of the Pentateuch, be they documents or layers, can be ordered based on their perceived literary or theological "maturity." A priestly community should be expected to have had a particularly cultic sensibility; those who were not priests, not so much—and this would be true at any stage of Israel's history. In today's world, the story of the founding of the United States, to take an easy and prominent example, comes out very differently depending on who is doing the telling. An author with a poet's sensibility will write in a manner easily distinguishable from, say, a lawyer (at least, a lawyer who is not also a poet). Conceptual difference, be it stylistic, ideological, or otherwise, does not require chronological development.

The notion of a singular redaction speaks to this. The Pentateuch is viewed not as a constantly growing corpus, each stage representing a new moment in Israelite thought, but rather as something like a literary warehouse for a wide range of contemporaneous ideas. It would be something of a surprise, and rather unprecedented, if the entirety of Israelite society—or even of

Israel's scribal elites—all held the same opinions, all told the same stories the same way, at the same time. The desire to fit sources, or layers, into a chronological conceptual scheme may be understandable, even natural, but it is not particularly true to life.

The historical reconstructions (religious, cultural, social/political) that have been based on the Pentateuch's literary history are thus also called into question by the neo-documentary hypothesis. The same is true for the historical circumstances that are often used as the basis for identifying and describing the purported layers of the text. If it is acknowledged that the documents all had their own lengthy histories prior to their combination, then the question of what it means to date a text at all is somewhat muddled. When someone first put pen to papyrus is not the "date" of a source; nor is the last time that a source was edited, if either can even be determined. At best we might be able to say that at some point in Israel's history someone thought x, y, or z. And though we might well imagine that a given text fits a particular moment better than another, that too falls into the category of speculation.[2] What the Pentateuch offers is a very broad view of the multiplicity of stories and theologies that existed in ancient Israel.

At the risk of oversimplifying, most of previous pentateuchal scholarship has fallen into two main (often overlapping) camps: the historical and the theological. The Pentateuch is taken to reflect Israel's history, and therefore it is an archaeological site from which historical knowledge can be extracted. Or the Pentateuch is

2. This was argued especially cogently by Benjamin Sommer in his essay "Dating Pentateuchal Texts."

viewed as a text whose meaning is accessible only when its compositional history has been established, when the context(s) of its creation are laid bare, and thus its true intentions made available. It is not that these are in any sense misguided or wrong as intellectual pursuits. But they each take a distinctive view of what the Pentateuch, and the Bible more generally, is: an encoded work, one that either holds the keys to the past or that requires a different sort of key to unlock it. In both cases, the text isn't just a text, and the question of its composition isn't really just about its composition.

If, according to the neo-documentary hypothesis, the Pentateuch is not what so many previous scholars have held it to be, then we might ask: so what is it? It is, first and foremost, a literary work, and it is in this light that neo-documentary scholars approach it. This may seem a rather meager statement, yet it is a crucial one. To take the Pentateuch as a work of literature is to ask literary questions of it—hence the focus on the way that the story is told, on the literary features of the canonical text that seem to demand some sort of explanation. Literary, rather than historical: not what the text might tell us about Israel's past, but why this piece of writing has to come to us in this unique and uniquely strange form. For all the textual analysis, most of previous scholarship has either used the Pentateuch's composition to access history, or used history to access the composition of the Pentateuch. For neo-documentary scholars, it is not that either of those is impossible (though both are more complicated than their practitioners tend to suggest). It is rather that those are simply not the primary tasks. The neo-documentary approach is, one might say, the English major's way to read the Pentateuch, not the historian's, and not the theologian's.

What is true of the whole is true of the parts as well. The isolation and definition of the sources is not intended to help reconstruct the history of Israel's development, along any potential axes. Rather, it seeks to retrieve ancient works of literature that have been obscured for millennia. One may do all sorts of things with those newly retrieved texts, but the first task, at least from the neo-documentary perspective, is to read them, to appreciate them as works of literary art. This allows them to speak for themselves: to be present to the reader on their own terms, rather than as a piece of some larger puzzle.

If, in the previous chapter(s), I suggested that there was perhaps something particularly Protestant about the ways that scholarship has typically approached the Pentateuch, it would be remiss here not to at least open the possibility that the neo-documentary hypothesis has a touch of Judaism to it. A text that preserves multiple voices simultaneously without prejudice toward any one of them, a text that is more receptacle than coherent argument—that's the Talmud, or the midrashic collections. Certainly the strong pushback against the antisemitism of Wellhausen's model, or what we might describe as the orientalism of the broader Romantic developmental theories, might be attributed to a similar Jewish sensibility. As virtually everyone we have discussed so far was a German Protestant, and the neo-documentary hypothesis emerged originally from Israel, this is perhaps not surprising. And, of course, to recognize certain religious or cultural inflections in a theory is not to say anything positive or negative about it per se; it is only to note that ideas do not emerge in a vacuum, and are often shaped by unconscious predispositions.

CASE STUDY. GENESIS 28:10–22 (SCHWARTZ [VIA BADEN])

The neo-documentarian analysis of the Bethel story, as is to be expected, focuses on the plot elements, isolating two distinct and internally coherent strands. Neither is a supplement or a redaction of the other; both are consistent with the narratives to which they connect. The J narrative is in plain text; E is in italics. I have slightly altered the translation in 28:11 and 28:20 to make the transition between the two sources clearer (though in the Hebrew there is no need for any adjustment).

> 10 Jacob left Beersheba and went toward Haran.
> 11 *He came to a certain place and stayed there for*
> *the night, because the sun had set. Taking one of*
> *the stones of the place, he put it under his head*
> *and lay down in that place.* 12 *And he dreamed*
> *that there was a stairway set up on the earth, the*
> *top of it reaching to heaven, and the angels of God*
> *were ascending and descending on it.* 13 And Yah-
> weh stood beside him and said, "I am Yahweh,
> the God of Abraham your father and the God
> of Isaac; the land on which you lie I will give to
> you and to your offspring, 14 and your offspring
> shall be like the dust of the earth, and you shall
> spread abroad to the west and to the east and to
> the north and to the south, and all the families
> of the earth shall be blessed in you and in your
> offspring. 15 Know that I am with you and will
> keep you wherever you go and will bring you
> back to this land, for I will not leave you until
> I have done what I have promised you." 16 *Then*

> *Jacob woke from his sleep* and he said, "Surely Yahweh is in this place—and I did not know it!" [17]*And he was afraid and said, "How awesome is this place! This is none other than the house of God, and this is the gate of heaven."* [18]*So Jacob rose early in the morning, and he took the stone that he had put under his head and set it up for a pillar and poured oil on the top of it.* [19]*He called that place Bethel, but the name of the city was Luz at the first.* [20]*Then Jacob made a vow;* and he said, "If God will be with me and will keep me in this way that I go and will give me bread to eat and clothing to wear, [21]so that I come again to my father's house in peace, then Yahweh shall be my god, [22][and] *this stone, which I have set up for a pillar, shall be God's house, and of all that you give me I will surely give one-tenth to you."*

The J story picks up in 28:10 directly from the end of the J story in Gen 27, where Rebekah instructs Jacob to flee to Haran (27:43). At an undisclosed (and narratively unimportant—for the moment) location, Yahweh appears to him, introduces himself, and gives him the standard J patriarchal promise, including the promise to watch over Jacob on his journey and return him to his native land (28:13–15). This too builds on the conflict between Jacob and Esau in J in Gen 27. Jacob's reaction is immediate: Yahweh is here. He then responds directly to the promise, though in what would appear to be an internal monologue, rather than a deal with Yahweh: If this deity—whom Jacob has not met before in J—will indeed do what he promised, then indeed Yahweh will be my god. It is likely that the first use of "God" in 28:20 was originally "Yahweh"; if so, this is probably a simple text-critical error rather than an intentional change.

The J story then continues with Jacob's journey to Haran, his (mis-)adventures there, and then his return. In Gen 31:3, Yahweh tells him to go back to his native land; in 32:10–13 Jacob recalls Yahweh's promise in 28:13–15 before he encounters Esau again; and in 35:1–7, Jacob goes back to this spot, now identified as Bethel: "Go to Bethel and remain there, and build an altar to the god who appeared to you when you were fleeing from your brother Esau" (35:1). This is as direct a reference to the J story in Gen 28 as one could hope for, and confirms the J elements as identified above: Jacob's flight from Esau and Yahweh's direct appearance to Jacob.

The E story makes no reference to Jacob's flight from Esau; indeed, in E the character of Esau never appears. This is merely an episode in Jacob's wanderings around Canaan. He comes to a certain place and spends the night there, where he dreams of the angels ascending and descending; upon awaking, he identifies the location as the "house of God," and when the sun rises he sets up the stone as a cultic pillar and calls the place Bethel ("house of God"). Having done so, he makes a vow: this pillar will eventually become a sanctuary, a house of God, and he will tithe there. The E story, then, is very much the etiology of the Bethel sanctuary, entirely contained within this episode.

Both stories participate in the same overall function, which is to explain the presence of a cultic site at Bethel. E does it here; J extends it over a broader narrative arc, in which it is Jacob's safe travel from and return to Canaan that confirm Yahweh's word and thus justify the construction of the sacred space. Nothing is missing from either story; each reads perfectly well on its own and in its broader source context. All of the sleeping and dreaming is in E;

all of the references to Jacob's flight, journey, and return, and Yahweh's being with Jacob, are in J. We can thus posit, along with Gunkel and Noth, a common underlying tradition of Jacob founding the sanctuary at Bethel, but we have no need to assume that both told the story in the same way, or even really at the same time.

In terms of how the two stories were combined, the redaction appears relatively straightforward. Jacob's departure from Beersheba in J (28:10) must precede his arrival at Bethel in E (28:11). Because he immediately sleeps in E (28:11), the dream (28:12) must come before Yahweh's direct appearance in J (28:13). This combination, however, makes it seem in the combined text as if Yahweh's appearance was also part of the dream. Thus Jacob does not wake until later (28:16). Jacob's two reactions are set in what seems a reasonably logical order, the inverse of his actual experience: Yahweh is here, and this is a special place (28:16–17). The E story continues until the notice of Jacob making a vow, at which point the two are combined again, logically enough: first Jacob sets the conditions, from J (28:20–21), then says what he will do in the future, from E (28:22). Every part of each source is maintained in its original order; nothing seems to have been removed from either; and there is but a single addition, entirely for grammatical purposes: the "and" at the beginning of 28:22, which links Jacob's vow from E with the preceding conditions from J.

The neo-documentary treatment of this passage thus, as one would expect, returns to the sources of generations past, but simplifies the analysis.

GUIDING QUESTIONS

1. How does the neo-documentary approach differ from earlier source-oriented models? How does it differ from Rendtorff's approach?
2. What is the relationship of literature and history in the neo-documentary theory?
3. In what ways does this approach simplify previous theories, and how does it allow for complications?

CONCLUSION

Source criticism—whether the name is apt or not—is a difficult field to dip one's toes into. With only a few brief exceptions over the past three centuries, there have always been multiple arguments being made simultaneously. Theories have changed, but often the various sigla used have remained constant. Thus what is labeled "J" in one work may not be the same "J" in another. Or, just as confusingly, sigla have changed, though the intended referent remains the same: depending on when a work was written, E and P might mean the same thing. And in the last fifty years, the two main approaches are so widely at odds, and the claims underlying them so often implicit or assumed, that the question of the Pentateuch's composition is almost inaccessible to the non-expert. This short book has been intended to provide those not deeply engaged in pentateuchal scholarship or source criticism—scholars, students, and lay readers alike—with an overview not only of what has been said but also, at least in part, of why it has been said.

It is my hope that in terms of the first piece—what has been said—this book will be a helpful guide for those who might pick up a work of source criticism and find themselves somewhat at sea. Though the history of the field is undeniably complex, there are usually good signs, should one pick up any work of scholarship, to indicate where the author stands. Does the work use "Urschrift" or "Grundschrift" to refer to the priestly texts? It's pre-Wellhausen. Does it use the term "JE" for the non-priestly texts? It's post-Wellhausen (but not present-day). Does it refer to J^1 and J^2? Early to mid-twentieth century, most likely. Does it use the terms "Hexateuch redaction" or "post-priestly layer"? It's from the last fifty years, and follows Rendtorff's approach. Does it use the term "compiler"? It's from the neo-documentary camp. Of course, one might also go the other way, and start not with what the scholarship says, but when it's from—and thus I similarly hope that this book provides a rough chronology into which a work of pentateuchal criticism can be fit. If one picks up a book from the mid-nineteenth century, one should thus expect to find that P—whatever siglum is used for it—is treated as the earliest of the pentateuchal writings. In a book from the early twentieth century, P will probably be the latest. In a book from the twenty-first century . . . well, it's either layers or sources, and one should be able to tell pretty quickly which it is.

I hope also to have shown that the various detailed analyses of the text are always influenced by wider trends, not only in the field of pentateuchal studies, or even biblical studies, but in the humanities more generally. The kinds of questions that are asked, and the kinds of assumptions that are brought, emerge not from the study of the Bible but from the broader cultural context. The traditional position of Mosaic authorship is not a textual claim but a confessional one. The move away from that position occurred in the context of the Enlightenment. The rise of Romanticism dramatically changed the way the Bible was read. Evolutionary theories, both scientific and philosophical, have had their impact. Studies of folklore and oral literature shifted the field. And so on. We can mark the moments that these trends first appeared on the scene, but it is also clear that very few of them have ever then gone on to pass from the scene entirely. They all remain with us, often implicitly, for better or for worse.

As for the "why," this is often much harder to recognize. Scholarship, past and present, tends to present itself as scientific, even if it is firmly in the humanities. Texts are analyzed, arguments are made, conclusions are reached, and for the most part the rationale behind even the initial question—why ask about the literary history of this text?—is unstated. I have therefore tried in the foregoing chapters to expose some of what I see as the underlying motivations behind the various approaches to the Pentateuch. Often, I imagine, the scholars and scholarship described above would not themselves be able to articulate some of these motivations. It is, admittedly, much easier to do this with the benefit of hindsight (though I have tried to also be somewhat introspective regarding my own positions). But it is our responsibility, I think, as scholars in the humanities, to always be attentive to how the theories being posited and the arguments being made reflect our own predispositions and presumptions.

This is especially so with the Bible, and perhaps even more particularly with the Pentateuch. At the root of every broad theory and every detailed analysis is an understanding of what this text is. Is it the word of God, or is it a human product? Is it authoritative, and if so, how, and to what extent, and when? Is it a work of history, revealing the past to us, either on the surface of the text or beneath it? Is it a work of literature? Is it the product of communities or individuals? Where is its meaning located: in the final form, in the earliest parts, or in the way that it was assembled, however that is imagined? Most analyses of the text don't engage directly in these questions. But a reader attuned to these questions will probably be able to discern at least some of the answers, and, I hope, with the help of this book will see how those answers come to shape the textual analysis.

Above all, perhaps, what I hope this book has done, in following the course of source-critical scholarship and especially in its attention to the "why" behind the "what," is to make clear that every argument, big or small, is always determined not by what is on the page of the Bible but what is in the head of the scholar. Every scholar and every approach described above is working with the same evidence, with the same words on the page. And we are all also working with the same lack of evidence. That is, every source-critical theory, from Mosaic authorship to the neo-documentary hypothesis, is speculative at best. It is of course possible that one is right; it is also possible that all are wrong. What makes a theory compelling is not (or not only) how well it explains whatever it is designed to explain (and this is not the same from theory to theory), but how well it conforms to the intellectual, and often theological, predispositions of the reader. I have suggested in the preceding chapters that some theories were popular precisely because they appealed to a certain Protestant attitude (and some perhaps because they appeal to a more Jewish sensibility). Some theories are designed to satisfy those who seek historical answers from the text; some for theological inquiry; some for the purely literary-minded. None of these is "right," per se. All are partial at best. The Pentateuch, and the Bible, cannot be "solved" by any one theory.

This is not to say that the attempt isn't worthwhile. This is, after all, the humanities—it isn't really our task to "solve" any problem. Every theory, every argument, provides further insight into the text and into the scholar. Source criticism, past and present, is a window onto the literary history of the Pentateuch and onto the intellectual history of those who study it. We continue to do the work because we still seek to understand this ever-fascinating and ever-troubling text—and we still seek to understand ourselves.

BIBLIOGRAPHY

Adler, Yonatan. *The Origins of Judaism: An Archaeological-Historical Reappraisal.* New Haven, CT: Yale University Press, 2022.

Astruc, Jean. *Conjectures sur les memoires originaux: dont il paroit que Moyse s'est servi pour composer le Livre de la Genese.* Brussels: Fricx, 1753. Reprint, Paris: Éditions Noèsis, 1999.

Baden, Joel S. *The Composition of the Pentateuch: Renewing the Documentary Hypothesis.* New Haven, CT: Yale University Press, 2012.

Blum, Erhard. *Die Komposition der Vätergeschichte.* Neukirchen-Vluyn: Neukirchener Verlag, 1984.

———. *Studien zur Komposition des Pentateuch.* Berlin: de Gruyter, 1990.

Carpenter, J. Estlin, and G. Harford-Battersby. *The Hexateuch according to the Revised Version.* New York: Longmans, Green, 1900.

Eissfeldt, Otto. *The Old Testament: An Introduction.* New York: Harper & Row, 1965.

Ewald, Heinrich. *Geschichte des Volkes Israel.* Göttingen: Dieterischen Buchhandlung, 1864–68.

———. *Die Komposition der Genesis kritisch untersucht.* Braunschweig: Ludwig Lucius, 1823.

———. Review of J. Stähelin, *Kritische Untersuchungen über die Genesis.* TSK 4 (1831) 595–606.

Fohrer, Georg. *Überlieferung und Geschichte des Exodus.* Berlin: de Gruyter, 1964.

Geddes, Alexander. *The Holy Bible; or the Books accounted sacred by Jews and Christians; otherwise called the Books of the Old and New Covenants; faithfully translated from corrected texts of the originals, with various readings explanatory notes and critical remarks*. London: R. Faulder and J. Johnson, 1792.

Graf, Karl Heinrich. *Die Geschichtlichen Bücher des Alten Testaments*. Leipzig: T. O. Weigel, 1866.

———. "Die s.g. Grundschrift des Pentateuchs." *Archiv für wissenschaftliche Erforschung des Alten Testaments* 1.4 (1869) 466–77.

Gunkel, Hermann. *Genesis*. Macon, GA: Mercer University Press, 1997.

———. *Genesis übersetzt und erklärt*. Göttingen: Vandenhoeck & Ruprecht, 1901.

———. *The Legends of Genesis*. Chicago: Open Court, 1901.

Harvey, Paul B., Jr., and Baruch Halpern. "W. M. L. de Wette's '*Dissertatio Critica . . .*': Context and Translation." *Zeitschrift für Altorientalische und Biblische Rechtsgeschichte* 14 (2008) 47–85.

Hupfeld, Hermann. *Die Quellen der Genesis und die Art ihrer Zusammensetzung*. Berlin: Wiegandt und Grieben, 1853.

Kaufmann, Yehezkel. *The Religion of Israel: Its Beginnings to the Babylonian Exile*. Chicago: University of Chicago Press, 1960.

Kugel, James L. *Traditions of the Bible: A Guide to the Bible as It Was at the Start of the Common Era*. Cambridge: Harvard University Press, 1998.

Legaspi, Michael. *The Death of Scripture and the Rise of Biblical Studies*. Oxford: Oxford University Press, 2010.

Levin, Christoph. *Der Jahwist*. Göttingen: Vandenhoeck & Ruprecht, 1993.

Morgenstern, Julius. "The Oldest Document of the Hexateuch." *Hebrew Union College Annual* 4 (1927) 1–138.

Nöldeke, Theodor. *Untersuchung zur Kritik des Alten Testaments*. Kiel, Germany: Schwers, 1869.

Noth, Martin. *A History of Pentateuchal Traditions*. Chico, CA: Scholars, 1981.

Pfeiffer, Robert. "A Non-Israelite Source of the Book of Genesis." *Zeitschrift für die alttestamentliche Wissenschaft* 48 (1930) 63–73.

Rendtorff, Rolf. *The Problem of the Process of Transmission in the Pentateuch*. Sheffield, UK: JSOT, 1977. Translation of *Das überlieferungsgeschichtliche Problem des Pentateuch*. Berlin: de Gruyter, 1977.

Simpson, Cuthbert. *The Early Traditions of Israel*. Oxford: Blackwell, 1948.

Smend, Rudolf. *Die Erzählungen des Hexateuchs und ihre Quellen untersucht*. Berlin: Reimer, 1912.

———. *From Astruc to Zimmerli*. Tübingen: Mohr Siebeck, 2017.

Sommer, Benjamin D. "Dating Pentateuchal Texts, or the Perils of Pseudo-Historicism." In *The Pentateuch: International Perspectives on Current Research*, edited by Thomas B. Dozeman, Konrad Schmid, and Baruch J. Schwartz, 85–108. Tübingen: Mohr Siebeck, 2011.

Spinoza, Baruch. *A Theologico-Political Treatise*. New York: Dover, 1951.

Vater, Johann. *Commentar über den Pentateuch*. Halle: Maisenhaus, 1802–5.

Volz, Paul, and Wilhelm Rudolph. *Der Elohist als Erzähler: Ein Irrweg der Pentateuchkritik?* Giessen: Töpelmann, 1933.

Von Rad, Gerhard. "The Form-Critical Problem of the Hexateuch." In *The Problem of the Hexateuch and Other Essays*, 1–78. New York: McGraw-Hill, 1966.

Wellhausen, Julius. *Die Composition des Hexateuchs und der historischen Bücher des Alten Testaments*. Berlin: Reimer, 1885.

———. *Prolegomena to the History of Israel*. Atlanta: Scholars, 1994.

www.ingramcontent.com/pod-product-compliance
Lightning Source LLC
LaVergne TN
LVHW051003080826
845145LV00009B/2425

* 9 7 8 1 6 6 6 7 6 4 0 9 3 *